ADVANCE PRAISE

"In this very insightful book, Dr. Jack Cochran dissects the evolving healthcare landscape while illuminating the essential role of the physician as a healer, leader, and partner. A great read for the public as well as all healthcare professionals."

—**RICHARD CARMONA**, MD, MPH, FACS, 17TH SURGEON GENERAL OF THE UNITED STATES, DISTINGUISHED PROFESSOR UNIVERSITY OF ARIZONA

"Jack Cochran has written another wise, sweeping and practical book that should be of interest to anyone concerned about the state of US health care. He asks physicians to add the roles of leader and partner—as members of complex health care delivery teams—to their more obvious identity and training as healers. To do this, Dr. Cochran draws from his own years of clinical experience, with humility and passion, to show what these new roles look like. The goal is the creation of learning communities that innovate and share best practices. Only by learning the skills of leadership, can physicians be equipped to navigate the complex journey ahead."

—**AMY C. EDMONDSON**, NOVARTIS PROFESSOR OF LEADERSHIP AND MANAGEMENT, HARVARD BUSINESS SCHOOL

"The book inspires on so many levels. First, there is practical and effective advice for physicians taking on new leadership roles, and the personal approach lays the path for adding new skills and approaches to leading in complex systems. Then, Jack Cochran defines the need and approaches to developing an effective learning system. We have so much variation across health care sites, and we desperately need to build effective ways to teach and learn. And the ideas in this book describe ways to define and nurture to a culture of caring and teamwork."

—**MAUREEN BISOGNANO,** RETIRED CEO OF THE
INSTITUTE FOR HEALTHCARE IMPROVEMENT

"Only Dr. Jack Cochran—a healer, leader, partner in his own right—could issue this clarion call for doctors to step to the front of the change movement in healthcare. With compassion, practicality, and a dose of self-deprecation, Dr. Cochran offers an inspiring vision for the future."

—**CECI CONNOLLY,** PRESIDENT AND CEO,
ALLIANCE OF COMMUNITY HEALTH PLANS

"In Healer, Leader, Partner, Jack Cochran distills his vast leadership experience into an accessible and actionable how-to guide that should be on the must-read list for clinical and business leaders and entrepreneurs alike. Among the many books that have been written about leadership, what stands out here is Dr. Cochran's ability to diagnose the underlying drivers of great leadership, identify common situational

symptoms to overcome, and prescribe concrete suggestions for understanding oneself, bringing together high performing teams, learning from failure, and achieving success. Clinical training and problem-solving, channeled in the right ways, do indeed have much to teach us about leadership within and beyond healthcare. Dr. Cochran's call to action is both inspiring and existential—we can and we must have the collective resolve to accept reality for what it is and create the healthcare system and future we all aspire to."

—JEAN DROUIN, MD, MBA, CEO AND FOUNDER, CLARIFY HEALTH SOLUTION

"Jack Cochran provides highly practical advice for leaders to inspire physicians and medical staffs. This book highlights the need for innovative systems and the critical components for transforming American Health Care. He leverages the lessons learned while serving at the helm of the nation's premiere physician-led healthcare organization, Kaiser Permanente. Jack concludes that physician leadership and the relationships with patients and staff are vital to achieve the highest quality and most effective healthcare. The insights provide important knowledge, capability and expertise and are presented in clear, accessible language. It is a must-read for all of us who are dedicated to providing the best in healthcare."

—RICHARD S. ISAACS, MD, FACS, CEO AND EXECUTIVE DIRECTOR, THE PERMANENTE MEDICAL GROUP, INC.; PRESIDENT AND CEO, THE MIDATLANTIC PERMANENTE MEDICAL GROUP; P.C., KAISER PERMANENTE

"Healer, Leader, Partner is a must-read for all healthcare professionals and anyone seeking to improve their leadership skills. Based on his experience as a physician, executive, and humanitarian, Cochran has written a book to help physicians navigate the ever-increasing complexity and change that is our technological, cultural, and political reality. Each chapter is stand-alone and offers mentoring and guidance toward the goals of intentional learning and of personal growth. It is a call-to-arms to transform healthcare, strengthen leadership, and enhance our accountability as compassionate healers. Every physician should purchase two copies—one for home and one for work."

—JANICE NERGER, DEAN OF THE COLLEGE OF NATURE AND SCIENCE, COLORADO STATE UNIVERSITY

"Jack Cochran was the leader he describes when he was at Kaiser-Permanente. Filled with practical, actionable, and timely wisdom for a struggling health care system, Healer, Leader, Partner is essential reading for leaders in health care or for that matter any organization that takes leadership— and the care of employees and customers—seriously."

—JEFFREY PFEFFER, THOMAS D. DEE II PROFESSOR OF ORGANIZATIONAL BEHAVIOR, GRADUATE SCHOOL OF BUSINESS, STANFORD UNIVERSITY AND AUTHOR OF *DYING FOR A PAYCHECK*

"A great leader in making healthcare better has written up his life learnings. The book is a summary of how doctors can lead

our never-ending quest for better healthcare, more affordable healthcare and more accessible healthcare. The book shows how doctors can lead change in this ambition. A must-read for doctors and non-doctors alike. And not one inch less relevant for countries other than the US!"

—**JOCHEM OVERBOSCH**, SENIOR PARTNER, CO-CHAIR OF GLOBAL HEALTHCARE, ODGERS BERNDTSON, AMSTERDAM

"Dr. Cochran's Healer, Leader, Partner challenges physicians and health leaders to think beyond the boundaries of their professional training and roles, to foster collaboration, to value the power of communication, and to lead creatively and with wisdom. Drawing on his experiences as a physician leader, he encourages reflection and a commitment to learning. In recent years, many Australian health leaders have had the privilege of Dr. Cochran's mentorship and have greatly valued his thoughtful insights, and his challenge to each of them to consciously aspire to active leadership. In Healer, Leader, Partner, Dr. Cochran draws together the themes he explores in his mentoring relationships, allowing these to be shared with a wider audience. This engaging, positive book offers lessons for all in health leadership roles."

—**ALISON VERHOEVEN**, CHIEF EXECUTIVE, AUSTRALIAN HEALTHCARE AND HOSPITALS ASSOCIATION

"This book creates hope. It is a fabulous addition to the body of knowledge on how to address the vexing challenges in

healthcare—drawing from years of experience and notable management theory to offer up not just a practical guide, but a compelling read. Jack weaves together masterful storytelling with a useful framework for self-reflection and change. He provides a thought-provoking set of values to guide behaviors and a clear call to action on how to achieve meaningful improvement. While aimed toward physicians, it will be of value to any and all who are part of the healthcare team. Jack inspires others to become more and do more as leaders and change agents."

—**NANCY PARKER TAYLOR**, VICE PRESIDENT OF STRATEGY, STANFORD SCHOOL OF MEDICINE

"Dr. Cochran has written a tour de force on physician leadership. His beautifully articulated lessons learned following years of thoughtful and dynamic impact should be required reading for aspiring and current physician leaders in order to optimize organizational success and facilitate the development of those around them. Going far beyond the reasons why physician leadership is critical, he gives physicians the critical building blocks and skillset necessary for leadership success. "

—**DR. MICHAEL BENTZ**, PROFESSOR AND CHAIRMAN OF PLASTIC SURGERY, UNIVERSITY OF WISCONSIN

"Jack's book reflects the truth of practicing as a physician in the 21st century. The complexity of health care today isn't the world many of us trained for in medical school, however *it is one we can lead in and find a sustainable career with, if we continue to learn, collaborate and mentor. We are in the midst of tremendous disruption and, as Jack so deftly outlines, our patients and the country needs physicians to embrace this opportunity to strongly influence the change during these transformational times.*

"I applaud Dr. Cochran's vision of physicians as leaders whether they are in an official leadership role, or working face to face with patients every day. And never have we needed physician leaders more than these times. Jack nimbly makes the case for physicians to be not only healers, but influencers, learners, collaborators and advocates for excellent, and critically, affordable care. And he recognizes the importance of investing in a fulfilling physician career that ultimately allows us to deliver better care to our patients."

—MARGARET FERGUSON, MD, PRESIDENT,
COLORADO PERMANENTE MEDICAL GROUP
OF KAISER PERMANENTE COLORADO

"Jack Cochran's book is not solely aimed at doctors; this fantastic book is for all of those with a passion for change and leadership. Healer, Leader, Partner looks at the complex demands being made on doctors as healthcare systems around the world are faced with greater challenges. Long has it been the status quo for doctors to take on the role of healer, however Jack explores the increasing demand for doctors to take on more holistic roles as both leaders and partners.

Written during my time as health minister, my 2008 report on the National Health Service in the UK, "High Quality Care for All," emphasised the importance of doctors not only being leaders but also partners for the greater benefit of the health system and for patients. This book explores this fundamental principle of clinical leadership, and touches on the challenges that both individuals and institutions face including cultural change. Throughout this engaging book, Jack's key message remains clear; to achieve high quality patient-centric care, physicians must embrace the roles of healer, leader and partner."

—THE LORD ARA DARZI OF DENHAM, PROFESSOR
OF SURGERY, IMPERIAL COLLEGE OF LONDON

"In Healer, Leader, Partner, Dr. Jack Cochran has once again stopped us in our tracks. In a world characterised by constant change and flux, he has come up with a calm, wise, practical road map for navigating the journey. The primary audience for this fine publication is his fellow physicians, faced with ever-increasing expectations, demands, complexities and costs. His answer for them is the embracing of Leadership and Partnership. But this is no Ivory Tower treatise, but rather a practical, accessible tool kit, rooted in his own lived experience as a renowned surgeon and Clinical Leader. And in the process, he has provided the rest of us from the non-medical world with unique insights into the nature of change and leadership more broadly. I feel sure this book will be an invaluable asset to physicians seeking to better equip them-

selves in discharging their critical mission and vocation in an ever more complex world; but it should also be required reading for anybody anywhere interested in understanding the anatomy of good and wise leadership."

—**TIM O'CONNOR**, CHAIRMAN, INTERNATIONAL CENTRE FOR LOCAL AND REGIONAL DEVELOPMENT

"Jack Cochran has written a timely and prescient book to prepare physicians to take up the challenge of transforming healthcare.

"I was struck by its relevance to leaders across the board, regardless of industry. My decades in corporate and institutional management have taught me managing change is a tough test of leadership; up there with managing conflict. Dr. Cochran discusses both. Contemporary institutions must reinvent themselves with accelerating frequency. This book says that axiom now applies to the doctor's office.

"Dr. Cochran's Healer, Leader, Partner is a sequel to The Doctor Crisis, his former book. It reflects his determination to continue to find solutions to a chaotic, expensive healthcare system by encouraging physicians, healers, to be part of the solution as leaders and partners. He referred to it as a manual, but it goes far beyond that. One could even think it should be an appendix to the current Hippocratic Oath."

—**ED JENSEN**, RETIRED PRESIDENT AND CEO, VISA INTERNATIONAL

"Jack is a practical visionary who has been a healer, leader, partner in his own high-impact career where he demonstrated effective leadership. His lessons are highly relevant to aspiring healers, leaders, and partners across healthcare as genomics, data, maths, and technology transform care. His thinking on partnership is relevant far beyond healthcare and applies to the world's largest partnerships in law and consulting as well."

—NICOLAUS HENKE, PH.D., SENIOR PARTNER, MCKINSEY & COMPANY (LONDON)

HEALER, LEADER, PARTNER

Nancy P —

Thanks for your encouragement, inspiration, and support!

Jack

HEALER
LEADER
PARTNER

OPTIMIZING PHYSICIAN LEADERSHIP
TO TRANSFORM HEALTHCARE

JACK COCHRAN, M.D.

LIONCREST
PUBLISHING

HEALER, LEADER, PARTNER

Optimizing Physician Leadership to Transform Healthcare

ISBN   978-1-5445-1127-6 *Hardcover*

978-1-5445-1128-3 *Paperback*

978-1-5445-1129-0 *Ebook*

*For Patients, Families, and **their** American dream!*

CONTENTS

KEY POINTS, VOLTAGE DROPS, AND WICKED QUESTIONS

Phrases, quotes, and sometimes paragraphs appear throughout this book labeled as Key Points, Voltage Drops, and Wicked Questions. For clarity, here are descriptions of each:

🔑 **Key Points** are brief, summary statements of important takeaway lessons or supporting messages from the key learnings in the chapter.

⚡ **Voltage Drops** are illustrations or examples of actions or behaviors that can undermine positive outcomes from an otherwise successful application of the lessons in the chapter.

❓ **Wicked Questions** are placed to stimulate thinking on the challenges presented in the chapter and to create focus on critical consequences.

PREFACE

MESSAGE TO MY PHYSICIAN COLLEAGUES

> **❓ WICKED QUESTION**
>
> Where will physicians be when health care is transformed?

Advances in medicine have enabled you, as a physician, to treat, relieve, and even cure many diseases. Your patients have trusted you and placed themselves under your care. The relationships you have with these patients are grounded in mutual understanding, open communication, compassion, and deserved trust. Clearly, your patients and the medical profession have benefited from so much progress and improvement. In so many ways, these positive changes are unquestionably what you hoped for when you pondered a career path as a physician.

For you, committing to becoming a physician was an enormous undertaking. The academic demand and rigor began early in school and continued through college, premed, medical school, residency, and fellowships. The relentless progress of the science and information in medicine also demanded a lifetime commitment from you. Being a physician required keeping your knowledge and skills up to the standards you—and others—expected.

You also had to commit to a work ethic, work habits, and the determination to devote a lifetime of long hours of work and ongoing learning. You had to be continuously available to respond when needed throughout the entirety of your practice. Your patients wanted you to be available, compassionate, knowledgeable, and up-to-date for their needs. Your skills, commitment, and professionalism were the keys to patients getting the kind of care they expected, needed, and deserved.

But during this same time period, while there have been many advances and improvements that ultimately benefited your patients—heavily enabled by your dedication and hard work—there have also been many other changes, disruptions, and intrusions. You didn't always like, agree with, or believe these were in the best interest of your patients. As a result, you may have become frustrated, angry, or disillusioned; some of your fellow physicians have even given up.

> ## 🔑 KEY POINT
>
> Health care is going to change regardless of our participation. If we opt out of engaging on major issues impacting our patients and families, we miss the opportunity to have a positive impact on their well-being.

This reality is why I wrote this book. I have seen superb, respected physicians give up and assume the role of victim, helplessly riding the wave of external decisions, policies, and regulations to a point of frustration and futility.

The fact that you are a doctor confers a very special role, opportunity, and accountability on your part. This unique position of trusted healer is an important platform for you to address the broader issues affecting patients in health care. Trust in your opinion continues to be at the top of the list for patients, and your clinical acumen and decisions have a disproportionate impact on their experience in so many ways. But like the role of victim, you must also not assume the role of tyrant and believe you can dictate the future.

Medicine is increasingly complex and requires good minds, information, technology, and teams to manage a system that your patients deserve. Make no mistake: you have surely seen physicians who became as self-focused as tyrants, and they may even create improvements, but too often at the expense of the culture—the soul and spirit of their teams and colleagues—to attain these short-term improvements. There is a higher path, one that is the most value-driven approach for physicians to comprehensively assume accountability for the breadth of their patients' contact with the system.

So here is the gap in your life: while patients need strong physician impact, broadly in the health system and in their care, you may feel beleaguered and powerless. You need tools, knowledge, and proven techniques to add "strong leader" to your toolbox in your practice, hospital, group, or organization. To project this enhanced sense of responsibility with the skills to be successful, let's look back at your own journey—a journey that started full of hope, energy, optimism, dedication, and idealism.

The academic challenges and rigor of your profession demanded your superb aptitude and ability, parlayed with discipline and hard work, to get your medical school application eligible for review. You had to personalize that application to let the admissions team understand why you, as an individual, a distinctive soul who also had outstanding grades, deserved the opportunity to take on the role of healer and physician. You had to write a couple of paragraphs about why you wanted to be a physician and why the covenant between you and those vulnerable patients was so dear to you. When you go back and reread these paragraphs, decades later, it can bring tears to your eyes, but it can also rekindle a flame to your rededication not only to continue to be a superb clinical doctor, but to devote yourself every day to being a leader in your medical community. The leadership taught in this book applies just as effectively to leading where you stand as a respected clinician, all the way to CMO or CEO. It is not about position but rather about a commitment to ensure that all patient issues have a physician's ear and hand in the understanding and solution.

To lead your profession and the patients' experience, you will need to develop the practical, proven, simple, but far-from-easy skills necessary to lead with values, compassion, authority, and impact.

You, physician, can be—you must be—a healer, a leader, and a partner.

Join up. It's your turn and it's your time. We need you.

PART I

PHYSICIAN AS HEALER

The covenant between patients and physicians is centered on the role of healer. Patients bring us their symptoms, pain, fear, and uncertainty for us to provide knowledge, care, relief, and compassion. They trust our ability to understand and care for them, and they hope for the compassion of the healer. Our ability to serve patients and families begins with this role of healer and the trusting relationship we develop and nurture.

But the reality of how broadly health care impacts patients and families has become more complex and challenging. While the role of healer must remain as the grounding of the relationship, we also need to honor and leverage this high ground to improve and transform health care by embracing and strengthening the mantle of leader and defining and enhancing the role of partner.

CHAPTER 1

WHY PHYSICIANS MUST LEAD

> ### ❓ WICKED QUESTION
>
> How do you get doctors to broaden their sense of
> responsibility to their patients?

As physicians, we are trained to diagnose and treat disease and relieve suffering. We dedicate ourselves, through rigorous training, to search for cures and perfect treatments and procedures to restore the health and wellness of our patients, and over the past few decades have made major progress from improvements, to miracles, and even cures. But our work is not done, and it needs to improve as patients still experience uneven quality, access, and affordability.

We must ask ourselves four questions.

1. IS EXCELLENT GOOD ENOUGH?

It seems clear that our interpretation of what is excellent today is not good enough for the future. Major progress has dramatically improved care in virtually all disease states. Following are just a few examples of this progress.

Heart disease: Major advances in drug therapies, interventional procedures, and devices to control rhythm and replace damaged structures have had widely positive impact. According to the American Heart Association, in 2017, the annual death rate attributable to coronary heart disease declined 35.5 percent from 2004 to 2014, and the death rate from stroke in that same period decreased 28.7 percent.

Cancer: Major advances in all modalities of therapy have improved results and some also reduced morbidity. According to the American Cancer Society, the cancer death rate peaked in 1991, with 215 cancer deaths per 100,000 persons; by 2015 that rate had declined by 25 percent, to 161 per 100,000.[1] Improvements in targeted therapies have emerged with great promise for more precise treatments, and this precision, at a molecular

---

1   *Cancer Facts and Figures 2017* (Atlanta: American Cancer Society, 2017).

level, enables therapies to be more specific for individual patients.

Surgery: We have seen steady improvement in the ability to do surgery with less invasive procedures, from minimally invasive techniques to endoscopic approaches, and to advances in the application of robotic techniques.

Combination Drug Therapies: Combination drug therapies beyond those used to fight cancer continue to evolve, such as those for treating HIV, TB, malaria, and other diseases.

Genomics: This field has experienced both continuous advances and some disappointments due to the early nature of its clinical use. The future, however, is both promising and exciting as we learn more details about the science and its potential clinical application.

Pharmacology: Pharmacology has added to a steady movement of "next generation" therapies in antibiotics, analgesics, anti-inflammatories, vaccines, and a diversity of therapeutic applications from pharmacotherapy.

Stem Cell Therapy: This rapidly evolving science may offer therapeutic improvements in many disease states and impact the normal degenerative processes.

Mathematics and Medicine: The rapid growth in technology, analytics, and the identification and classification of massive amounts of data and information are transforming both diagnostics and selection of therapies. The application of data analytics, algorithms, artificial intelligence, and machine learning can exceed the skills of the most highly functioning human brain but, I will argue, not replace the role of trusted clinician.

While this is not an exhaustive list, it is important to note that anti-smoking legislation, seat-belt legislation, and driving-under-the-influence enforcement all have had a major impact.

However, we continue to struggle with uneven quality results, inequity, problems with access, and a growing challenge with affordability. We also see disturbing trends in obesity, addiction, violence, and disparities in our communities.

In fact, medical error is still the third-leading cause of death in the United States,[2] surpassed only by heart disease and cancer, respectively. And personal bankruptcy from medical bills is the number two cause of bankruptcy for families in the United States. Families are not waiting

---

2   Vanessa McMains, "Johns Hopkins Study Suggests Medical Errors Are Third-Leading Cause of Death in U.S.," *John Hopkins University Hub*, March 3, 2016, accessed November 9, 2017, https://hub.jhu.edu/2016/05/03/medical-errors-third-leading-cause-of-death.

for the ideal legislation or the perfect insurance plan. All they want is affordable access to safe care. This leaves us to answer the question, "Is excellent good enough?"

This leads to the second question.

2. WHAT KIND OF ANCESTORS WILL WE BE?

This question is a rephrasing of Dr. Jonas Salk's quote, "Our greatest responsibility is to be good ancestors."

When I started practicing as a surgeon, health care costs were 10 percent of our GDP, and they are now 18 percent. During this time, I believe I have delivered a lot of quality care in a compassionate and caring manner, and I have also prospered professionally, personally, and financially. But what about my eleven-year-old grandson, Taylor? He will inherit an obligation for my Medicare and Social Security from my large generation of baby boomers. This 18 percent is an absolute reality that is being transferred to our future friends and family.

Wealth transfer into health care negatively impacts families, businesses, and governments. The impact on government is at all levels and is in the news daily. At a national level, it impacts total government spending and national debt.

This wealth transfer also impacts business in many ways.

One is in their basic costs. General Motors spends more per car on health care costs than they do on steel. That is a major factor, especially in global markets. The second major impact on business links directly to the individual employee and their family in two ways: health care cost mitigation has been realized by some employers by no longer covering the family of the worker but only covering the worker. The other tension is the spending of salary and benefit dollars on employees. When that money is examined, there can be a tough choice between keeping up with health care inflation and any wage increase.

Finally, there is the reality of the average American family. Families want to care for themselves, and health care is a major issue. As the cost of monthly health insurance premiums continues to rise, one adaptive behavior for families is choosing coverage with a higher deductible, betting they will never have to pay it. Unfortunately, this is a gamble that, if lost, could amount to thousands of dollars of unexpected costs when a family member suddenly becomes sick or is in an accident.

Because of this, average families are forced to ration health care every month.

It is common for a family to be facing competing needs for an MRI, paid out of pocket, and a new clutch on a truck that is needed for a parent to work, or an

elective procedure versus a new refrigerator. Many families don't have this discretionary family budget readily available anyway, so they opt for deferral, difficult decisions, or credit cards. These options are tough on family reality, *so they must ration health care at the kitchen table.*

Contrast these realities with the reality of physicians. On the one hand, we have the trust of patients to give the right advice and deliver the right care safely. And the decisions to deliver care are still made mostly by the patients and their physicians—up to eighty-three cents of every dollar is still spent on health care directly. As a group, we have a concerning number of physicians who are burned out or disillusioned at this time when we are needed to lead this very large challenge. Therefore, we must include a strong commitment to learning how to address the issues that are negatively impacting the career satisfaction and enthusiasm of a growing number of unhappy physicians.

So, we must entertain the third question.

3. HOW BIG IS OUR AMBITION?

Over the past several decades of medical advances, we have been able to deliver wonderful care to relieve many patients through some very challenging times. And yet, we have some real problems inside the house of medicine that are challenging not only us, as professional healers, but also vulnerable individuals with families and with many responsibilities. It is obvious that the current system is not optimal. Can we reasonably trust this system will be corrected by the status quo and others with no clinical awareness?

In times of change learners inherit the earth; while the learned find themselves beautifully equipped to deal with a world that no longer exists.

—ERIC HOFFER

Despite a physician cohort that is unhappy and some that are even disillusioned, we must never forget that honored covenant we have with patients. *The role of patient is involuntary*, and they need us more than ever.

As healers, we must always be focused on outstanding clinical care delivery, as that is our platform of credibility from which we can embrace being compassionate, patient-centered leaders who boldly commit to transforming our health care system for patients, families, and, frankly, the bigger American dream.

Patients encounter the health care system physically, socially, psychologically, and financially. In addition to being a superb physician clinically in any specialty, we must embrace the roles of healer, leader, and partner because these roles combine to fully acknowledge and support the complexity of the patient's reality.

Today, business leaders and employers, aware of this situation and its effect on their employees, are getting involved. A *New York Times* article about business magnate Warren Buffet noted, "Mr. Buffett said our global competitiveness had fallen largely because our businesses were paying far more for health care—a tax by another name—than those in other countries." The article went on to quote Buffet as saying, "Medical costs are the tapeworm of American economic competitiveness." Buffet was making a point that health care costs, and not corporate taxes, were crippling business.[3]

As we have reviewed and documented, there is a discrepancy between all the data around advances in health care and the ongoing problems surrounding evenness of quality. Problems with access and affordability have, on occasion, made health care very challenging for the average patient and family. We need to change this trend and create an inflection point where all the impacts of health care begin to align in a positive direction with the needs of our patients and families.

---

3   Andrew Ross Sorkin, "Forget Taxes, Warren Buffett Says: The Real Problem Is Health Care," *New York Times*, May 8, 2017, accessed February 16, 2018, https://www.nytimes.com/2017/05/08/business/dealbook/09dealbook-sorkin-warren-buffett.html.

People are still having trouble with this system, and we've got to stop that trend and work toward improving access and affordability. If health care impacts a family in ten ways, and six of them are positive and four of them are negative, physicians have got to create an inflection point so that we are not only solving individual clinical issues but also the totality of the problems patients have encountering the health care system. That is the inflection point.

Finally, the fourth question we as physicians must ask ourselves.

4. HOW BROAD IS OUR SENSE OF PERSONAL MISSION?

Can we commit to the health of our entire communities by leading the journey to Learning Communities? This is a major step toward health care becoming a true Learning Industry, and it means we must continue to optimize the performance of our own organization through excellent outcomes. Additionally, we must also commit to collaboration with other organizations including direct competitors to find solutions for the entire community beyond our organization. The dilemma we must face is examining the scope of our responsibility. Does it include simply our subset of customers/patients, or should our scope of responsibility be expanded to the entire community? This forces us to examine the place of competition versus collaboration expressed as keeping competitive advantages to ourselves, rather than embracing collaboration and generous sharing with competitors in order to drive improvement in the greater community.

A good example of a grassroots learning coalition movement is the Choosing Wisely campaign originated by the American Board of Internal Medicine, which has been expanded by a broad coalition of learning organizations that continue to work together to advance the best science to make the most sensible decisions in selecting care options. This is a true Learning Coalition dedicated to patient-centered discussions to optimize quality, safety, access, and affordability.

A great example of community collaboration is the work done by the multiple major hospitals in the city of London around stroke care. The decision to develop a national stroke strategy was made, and a process was completed that changed the model from an open referral system to thirty-two hospitals, to a focused and resourced system of eight hyper stroke units with more robust resources and capabilities. The results for stroke patients continue to demonstrate improved outcomes, including fewer complications and deaths and better functional results. This very intentional process meant that a large number of hospitals no longer delivered this kind of care to create a better outcome for the community at large.

The decisions made in London required a collaboration focused on the total needs of the community versus the individual business of each hospital. This is hard work but it is essential.

THE CHARGE FOR PHYSICIANS TODAY

Patients need physicians to lead where we stand. We need to embrace the roles of healer, leader, and partner, and become part of a physician workforce that's a little better for the American patient. We can rise to the challenge with more emotional intelligence, be more savvy in dealing with demanding situations to help our patients, and embrace a broader awareness of our accountability and choosing to opt in. Often, that accountability and the ability to affect change extend beyond the examination or operating room and beyond the healer role.

Physicians must begin to embrace a holistic view of the total impact of health care on patients, and how families have to worry about cost, access, and complications of care all the time—not just in the clinical moment when the patient is facing us in the exam room or operating room.

HEALER

If you look at the roles individually, being a healer doesn't take any more time or effort in your day as a physician. Here, your mindset is, "I understand the fear. I understand the uncertainty. I understand what's going through your (the patient's) mind, and all of those things you're worried about." The physician as healer is just a little quieter, more mindful, and more attentive, and understands that there must be a certain sensitivity and kindness to the doctor-patient interchange. It is a mindset and a commitment.

If you want to see a perfect example of a healer, head into your waiting room and look at one of your receptionists. They are sitting there, face-to-face with all that pain, peril, and uncertainty exuding from your patients, and your receptionist has no clinical tools to treat them, cure them, or even ease the pain. All they can do is listen, be kind, and maybe get them a little water and sit with them. They may not be physicians with the skills needed to cure the patient, but they understand the mindset and the commitment of healer, and they practice it every single day.

Again, as fully accountable physicians being fully responsible to patients and their needs, we must embrace the roles of healer, leader, and partner. This doesn't mean that you don't start off by being a great orthopedic surgeon, family doctor, or OB/GYN, because you must start there. A physician healer, leader, and partner also recognizes the complexity of the patient's reality, the care team, and the system of care surrounding the patient.

LEADER

This role may be new to some and well-known to others, but I believe the role of physician as leader must be part of the future solutions for all the complex ways patients encounter our system. Physicians as leaders must comprehensively opt in on behalf of patients for all the ways the system impacts them, including quality, access, equity, affordability, and safety. If you pursue a track of full-time clinical care, you are still a leader based on your professional credibility and your unwavering awareness of all the ways patients are impacted by the system. You must lead wherever you stand to fulfill your covenant with patients. I believe this book can provide some important learnings and insights for you.

Others may find that more involved or formal leadership may be desirable, and I believe this book can be a true manual of straightforward learning and encouraging lessons for your journey. This leadership development journey will require investment of time and budget to ensure that physician leaders have the training, development, support, and time to be effective.

Traditionally, physicians do not view the issue of health care affordability as part of their job. Some believe that affordability can diminish the devotion to quality, which it does not and should not. Consider this, from Jim Kouzes and Barry Posner: "To us, leadership is everyone's business. Leadership is not about a position or a place. It's an attitude and a sense of responsibility for making a difference."[4] That sense of responsibility demands a willingness to partner with patients instead of seeing ourselves as powerless victims standing on the sidelines, waiting for things to get better. Power doesn't only come from CEOs, CMOs, DMOs, or Deans, and, if you think that way, you will tend to opt out of this responsibility—this ability—to affect change.

A very insightful assessment of the deficiencies in physician leadership development was experienced by General Mark Hertling, who retired in 2013 from four decades

---

4   James M. Kouzes and Barry Z. Posner, *Encouraging the Heart: A Leader's Guide to Rewarding and Recognizing Others* (San Francisco: Jossey-Bass, 2003).

as a distinguished US army officer. Lieutenant General Hertling's stellar reputation as leader caused him to be recruited as a senior vice president at Florida Hospital with a major responsibility to develop leadership with a focus on physicians. His early findings, presented in his book, *Growing Physician Leaders*, were summarized in this early paragraph:

> Soon after I signed on, the chief operating officer and chief medical officer began a conversation with me about the topic of leadership. Both men had for a long time wanted to find ways to help doctors become better leaders so they could more effectively contribute to the culture of the organization, yet both admitted they hadn't found the right approach or the right program. They had tried sending physicians to a variety of courses at other organizations. That tactic didn't work. They contracted for consultants to work as coaches with specific physicians currently in leadership roles. That approach didn't get them the results they needed, either.[5]

Hertling's conclusion was, "I see little opportunity for physicians to learn how to lead," and when he asked the physicians for their view on this training, he discovered that "they protest that while they have no difficulty finding schools of management or business administration

5   Mark Hertling, *Growing Physician Leaders: Empowering Doctors to Improve Our Healthcare* (New York: RosettaBooks, 2016), 2.

that offer instruction on processes, systems, negotiation, communication skills, and the like, they've looked in vain for potent, organized approaches that teach and train the basic principles of leadership."[6]

Later, after describing some essential skills, Hertling noted that "as basic to accomplished leaders as some of these skills are, most of these techniques—setting standards, counselling, encouraging teamwork, rewarding performance, and challenging one's organization—are never discussed in formal medical school training."[7] So, while they are framing the issues and creating vigorous training solutions, the issues are pervasive.

The October 2017 issue of the American Medical Group Association's *Group Practice Journal* presented an article titled "The 'Lost Population' in Pop Health: Five Strategies to Engage Physicians in Your ACO,"[8] which documents the learning journey of an organization trying to transform itself and the challenges of bringing physicians along. The powerful lesson is that you can be a physician who doesn't have an official leadership role or title, yet still change the way an operating room works

6   Hertling, *Growing Physician Leaders*, 5-6.

7   Hertling, *Growing Physician Leaders*, 137.

8   Larry Allen, MD, "The 'Lost Population' in Pop Health: Five Strategies to Engage Physicians in Your ACO," *American Medical Group Association*, October 13, 2017, 10, accessed December 27, 2017, https://www.amga.org/Store/detail.aspx?id=GPJ_ART_1017_10.

by your actions, demeanor, and how you handle difficult situations. You can sit on the sidelines and let things play out, or you can take the lead—you don't need a special title to do that.

The physician's role as leader requires commitment too, and it requires some investment. Our patients encounter the system in so many ways, stretching well beyond the time they spend with us in the exam room or the operating room. And so, we cannot absolve ourselves of responsibility for issues around access or affordability, or problems our patients are having with the hospital or other health system. If we continue to delegate all the major leadership functions in health care to others, then we will continue the current trend of being on the sidelines, watching things happen to us and around us instead of taking an active role in that patient's total health care experience.

At a system level, an investment of time is required. You can't be the chief of surgery and just show up to a meeting the first and third Thursday night of the month—perhaps to participate in the quality committee one night and the executive committee on the other night—and call yourself a leader. Leadership roles must be supported and developed, and there's an investment required. You can't simply tack on a meeting at the end of the day. Leaders require time to lead. They require training and mentoring specific to the discipline of leadership. It's not a two-nights-a-month job.

PARTNER

Finally, the physician as partner understands and embraces the fact that health care has become a team sport. In other words, you are not an individual contributor working in your own silo and oblivious to the rest of the players. As physician, you have a disproportionate impact and a lot of power regarding the patient's health care experience. You have a lot of influence on the team. You set the tone and have a hand in the culture. If your team, which includes other doctors, nurses, and other medical staff, is working hard to raise the bar in health care, you have a responsibility to align with their aspirations and goals. If you've set the bar too low, and your team is saying, "We'd like to do better, but Dr. Cochran is a jerk. He doesn't want to do better, and he doesn't care what we want, or even think," then you—or I, in this example—can't expect anyone else to rise to the occasion. I have defined how far we can go and how good we can be by my own behaviors, actions, and limitations.

🔑 **KEY POINT**

Beyond integration, there must be alignment.

No individual or group can make an optimal contribution to create a sustainable solution in health care by primarily focusing on their own agendas and needs.

Medicine has its roots in individual education, training, practice, and existence. But we will talk about the overwhelming impact of complexity, and how much medicine now requires collaboration, cooperation, and connected learning, which are all partnership activities.

Developing the awareness and ability to be a strong partner benefits physicians in many situations. Within their role, they may: (1) be responsible for the difficult comanagement of a complex patient; (2) be tasked with leading a strategic process to deliver orthopedic care; (3) be expected to work with legislature to ensure that the patient and clinician views are understood; (4) have to work with IT to optimize the efficacy of an IT solution; and (5) take on the responsibility of overseeing negotiations with a labor union. The power of collaboration, cooperation, and aligned decisions is essential to leverage the larger challenges facing health care.

As physicians, our responsibilities must expand. We must be willing to take on issues in health care such as affordability and quality, and problems beyond the examination room and the operating room. We must also educate ourselves, not necessarily with an MBA, MPH, or any other degree, certification, or academic exercise, but by developing a new skill and mindset that complements our medical training. We must embrace the role of healer, leader, and partner, and approach these roles with the same commitment and generosity of spirit with which we signed up to become physicians so many years ago.

In *The Doctor Crisis*, which I coauthored with Charles C. Kenney, we track the pathway of the physician profession-ally over the last several decades to understand how that has tracked with all the changes in health care generally.[9]

As physicians, we come from an academic discipline of precision and science, so we are naturally skeptical. We expect proof to consider the possibility of new informa-tion that challenges our beliefs, and we only accept with confirmation. That skepticism is a natural reality for a scientist to be certain that the high bar of truth is realized before we consider it as part of our professional knowl-edge base.

Highly respected Harvard surgeon and author Dr. Atul Gawande studied many major advances in medicine over the last century in an effort to understand why some were

---

9   Jack Cochran and Charles C. Kenney, *The Doctor Crisis: How Physicians Can, and Must, Lead the Way to Better Health Care* (Philadelphia: Public Affairs, 2014).

quickly embraced and spread while others were spread much more slowly or inconsistently. He compared the discoveries of anesthesia and antiseptics, both of which were major advances in safety and quality of care delivery. The adoption of anesthesia happened quickly and globally. The adoption of antiseptics was much slower and inconsistent for a long time. Gawande posited about the differences, noting, "First, one combatted a visible and immediate problem (pain); the other combatted an invisible problem (germs) whose effects wouldn't be manifest until well after the operation. Second, although both made life better for patients, only one made life better for doctors."[10] In fairness, I would argue that any negative outcome for patients ultimately impacts physicians negatively.

Gawande reviewed other advances to understand why the variation in adoption and the learnings were not simple and easily categorized. One theme he discussed was the emphasis on how and what to do to spread change, which did not always work. He alluded to the impact of why in the process. He also mentions the work of Everett Rogers on diffusion of information. We will discuss both important themes in detail in chapter 9, "Leading Change."

---

10 Atul Gawande, Slow Ideas, *The New Yorker*, July 29, 2013, accessed January 22, 2018, https:// www.newyorker.com/magazine/2013/07/29/slow-ideas.

Let's look at our traditional path to understand how change has impacted the profession and the individual physician and patient.

WHAT HAS CHANGED?

Choosing a medical career is a sizable commitment. We must work hard to ensure we attain a strong college education and performance record to be considered alongside many equally motivated and dedicated students. We need strong transcripts, references, and scores on the Medical College Admission Test (MCAT). In addition, we are required to write a short essay on why we want to be a physician and what that will mean to us.

If you go back and read those paragraphs that you wrote, you will find them teeming with idealism and a desire to serve and heal. For some, reading that essay many years later can be a very emotional moment—emotional because of the contrast with our current daily reality and mindset. Too many are very unhappy with the profession and their reality and can't identify with the twenty-one-year-old idealist who wrote that essay. They still believe it is an honorable profession and a high calling, but up to 60 percent are not sure they would enter the profession again or encourage their child to become a physician.

How did we get here?

I won't track every detail of the last several decades but observe the key changes and how they changed the practice of medicine for physicians and patients. And I want to make the case for physicians to lead the future from the professional platform of key trusted clinician and caregiver (healer), which is a platform that was hard earned and must now be leveraged to create a better future for patients and all the professionals who care for them.

WHAT ABOUT THE NURSES?

Does writing a book focused on strengthening physician leadership capability overlook the important contributions made on behalf of patients by nurses, pharmacists, and other team members? My answer is no, for two reasons.

First, the explicit expectation of physicians to emulate all three roles of healer, leader, and partner is designed to acknowledge and elevate the importance of patients, nurses, pharmacists, and all members of the team. There is no intent to advance physicians' careers and lives in any way that would diminish the concern for and importance of all these individuals. In fact, all should benefit by this broader sense of accountability.

Second, I believe this book can be beneficial reading for all health care professionals to increase their capabilities and confidence. In an ideal work environment, every health care professional can make major contributions by embracing the skills and roles of healer, leader, and partner.

The roots of medicine were based on a simple relationship between doctor and patient, where the doctor had most of the important and necessary information and treatment options and patients had their needs met via that relationship. In those days, most doctors were broadly practicing, primary care physicians with a good medical education and a small amount of post-graduate training. There were few journals, few randomized clinical trials, few educational meetings, no internet, and a limited set of diagnostic and therapeutic options. The computer with the essential information was the human brain, and the options for treatment were somewhat limited. Payment was in cash or the earliest forms of employer support. We need to understand what has happened but very importantly understand how we acted and reacted to see how to create a different future.

Fast-forward to today and I will briefly describe two waves of complexity that have happened and have forever changed much of our reality and created the platform from which the future will be forged...by us or to us.

The first wave of complexity is in information, technology, scientific advancements, and the business of medicine. I have mentioned these pervasive changes, including therapeutic breakthroughs in pharmacotherapy, surgery, diagnostics, and evolving therapeutic innovations in the clinical armamentarium.

We have also seen, at warp speed, the opportunities to

learn from the enormous amount of data present in the world through the application of analytics, algorithms, artificial intelligence, and so on. This flow of information benefited the subspecialists of each organ system: cardiologists, pulmonologists, and so on.

With increased complexity, the consequences to primary care became clear. Primary care physicians had to depend more on the depth of subspecialty knowledge and support and needed to stay well-connected with both their patients and the subspecialist.

THE INDUSTRIAL AGE VERSUS THE INFORMATION AGE

The preindustrial period in medicine had very limited information about medicine and disease and offered limited therapies. The use of purging, chanting, blood-letting, and sunshine did little to stem illness, and death rates were high.

The Industrial Age and development of machines and manufacturing enabled major advances in science and technology. In medicine, there was great progress in knowledge and capabilities with important and impactful improvements in a broad range of both diagnostic and therapeutic modalities.

The primary method of delivering medical care was the one-on-one, doctor-patient visit within that trusting and compassionate relationship. The knowledge, decisions, actions, and power were all centered on this visit.

Physicians read books and journals and attended conferences to stay current and to continue to be the reliable source of clinical information. The primary sources of knowledge and information were the physician's brain and the paper chart.

But as the Information Age of medicine advances, major changes and impacts have occurred, rendering the capacity of the physician's brain and the paper chart insufficient to solve many of today's clinical problems. For example:

1. Exponential growth in knowledge, information, and technology in many forms
   a. Pervasive growth and adoption of IT as an essential tool in all activities and learning
   b. Individuals globally have increased their competency, expectation, and dependence on technology

2. Medical breakthroughs and success
   a. Successful treatment of acute conditions may result in a chronic condition
   b. All clinical advances have the potential to extend life with the eventual development of additional conditions
   c. Even successful therapies that cure a primary condition may have side effects and toxicities, resulting in new problems

That's the Information Age, where we use knowledge, information, data, technology, algorithms, and various tools and teams to deliver a much broader population base. It's a very different model, and it doesn't lend itself to physicians being completely in charge, in their office, with all the data in their brain. The Information Age, because of its complexity, requires data, technology, analytics, and teams, and that's a bridge not all physicians are traversing easily or readily or happily.

The sum total of all these changes is significant increases in complexity that far exceed the powers of the human mind.

The good news is the same factors that have enabled much of this complexity are also the capabilities that not only solve the associated problems, but also provide powerful tools to develop more innovative and effective methods of care.

Where these challenges are being successfully confronted, the system of delivering care looks quite different, and the learning in this space is evolving rapidly.

Rather than a paper chart and a keen human brain, Information Age care delivery deploys collaborative teams using cutting-edge technology and a steady flow of tools and platforms that harmonize these forces. The use of IT, analytics, big data, algorithms, and dynamic care pathways with real-time monitoring are revealing a new frontier of learning that can answer Information Age questions.

- Old Question: How many patient appointments can you serve?

- New Question: How many patients' problems can you solve?

- Old Question: How do you convince patients to get recommended prevention?

- New Question: How do we create a system of tracking and clinical evidence that optimizes patients getting recommended prevention?

- Old Question: How often should a physician see a patient to monitor a condition?

- New Question: What is the best way to use home monitoring, personal devices and data, and members of the team to monitor a condition?

The future is very bright if we accelerate the acceptance of the necessity of embracing the possibilities of technology and team care and learn rapidly across our different organizations.

Growth in external industries such as pharmaceutical and device development, the legal system, lobbying organizations, financial schemes, and fraud and abuse are all realities. The increase in depth and sophistication of knowledge in clinical medicine pushed each clinical specialty to further subspecialize to maintain a current depth of competence: cardiology branched into invasive, interventional, vascular, valve, electrophysiology, and so on.

The dependency on the human brain also became more difficult. The addition of the computer as support was very challenging to the practice, habits, and routines throughout medicine, but it meant that for the physician, clinical autonomy was not what it used to be, and physicians had to learn to collaborate and cooperate more with a team centered on and supporting the patient. This is an example of physician as partner.

Payment for health care has changed dramatically and created new realities for physicians and new challenges well beyond "do an excellent job for the patient in front of you and get a fair payment." Inflation has created many of our hardest issues to solve. Health care inflation can be silent, like undiagnosed high blood pressure. The impact and progress are relatively unnoticed until a major event occurs.

The second wave of complexity has paralleled the first with different implications for the delivery of care and design of care delivery. With this wave is a complexity of patients, where patients began living longer, surviving one illness and then contracting a second or a third one, so the knowledge around one disease or one diagnosis became insufficient. The added interaction of diseases and therapies added more complexity.

This second wave changed the roles for primary care and specialty care. In the first wave of complexity, the subspecialist was very central because every disease required the depth and the complexity of their knowledge. When people started surviving heart problems and then got other illnesses, the cardiologist was no longer primarily in charge, and no longer the only subspecialist physician to that patient. A group of subspecialists trying to take care of a patient introduces new issues not solved simply by each individual being competent and attentive, so the second wave of complexity emphasizes the primary care doctor as the chief coordinator of the patient's journey through all these other subspecialty care connections. This role of coordinator of the patient's journey was also a key role in the first wave for primary care, but this new level of complexity anchors the need for primary care to be at the center, with the patient.

Someone had to manage the overall care, and the potential for incompatibilities of combined care and reactions of combined medicine provided by the subspecialists. This change in complexity was, in a sense, an essential role of primary care: to be at the center of the care team alongside the patient, to not only oversee complex care processes but also convene specialists when needed, interpret complex messages for patients, and add the art of collaboration to the care process. Primary care is now essential to optimize patient care in the face of both waves of complexity, and the attendant technology and information requires strong physician input.

The primary care doctor had to accept the fact that some patients have illnesses in which they don't have a great depth of knowledge; however, they are still smart, knowledgeable, and competent doctors who are very valuable to patients as the interpreter, explainer, and mediator. The primary care physician had to give up the notion that they know all that is necessary to treat a patient and, although they at times are still the pilot, they also, for multiple complex patients, must be the air traffic controller.

A growing number of patients are affected by this second wave, due to the large population of aging baby boomers and because current and advancing therapies are keeping this cohort alive longer, allowing this group to inevitably develop maladies of other organ systems.

These first and second waves have led to medical advancements and success in care. The medical industry has become so advanced because of the scientific progress resultant from the first wave of complexity that patients are cured or successfully treated more often, but this situation is not without consequences. People continue to live with the diseases that at one time were fatal and may now develop a problem with another organ system.

These patients with multiple organ system problems can no longer be cared for only by deeper subspecialization, and this level of complexity begins to clarify what the future will hold. No individual physician of any specialty can handle individuals in the growing cohort. The solutions here are patient-centered, IT-enabled, and knowledge-supported team care, and the center of the team is the patient with their trusted primary care physician (healer) connected and collaborating with the associated specialists (partner) and always working with the health care team, hospital, and community to continuously learn and improve care and outcomes (leader).

My belief is that the reality today is prime for physicians to lead more and better in the future while embracing the roles of healer, leader, and partner.

This increasing complexity of knowledge, technology, information, and how patients demand care has accelerated development of Information Age solutions leveraging technology, associated tools, information, and analytics. These are the key enablers to developing teams partnered and focused on the needs of patients as individuals and populations. The complexity cannot be solved by linear solutions, but demands integration and coordination from diverse sources, requiring managing relationships with good support by accessible information.

TRANSFORMING HEALTH CARE INTO A LEARNING INDUSTRY

We need to make health care a learning industry. The inflection point won't come from one bright leader or one superb organization. We have a wide range of interconnected issues in health care. We can spend time blaming various parts of the industry for these challenges, or we can realize that we can influence and accomplish much by working and learning together. We need talented people of deep expertise in specialized areas and, at the same time, an understanding of the broader impact of their actions. We need to draw from all parts of the industry, harnessing our collective knowledge for the practice of medicine, for the pharmaceutical industry, and for medical research, as well as a variety of other disciplines such as policy, economics, and engineering. We can only achieve this inflection point by being good partners, interconnecting, working collaboratively, and learning together. We can't treat or legislate our way out of this crisis; we must learn our way out of it.

To truly leverage learning, improvement, and innovation in our global industry, we need to elevate collaboration and learning almost to the same level as we place business results and success. Health care is a global business with solutions to be found around the world. A commitment to collaboration and learning can help us create that inflection point in health care and can also improve our business success.

By building a learning coalition, we can learn from challenges and successes across the health care industry. The innovations that can transform our industry are out there; they're just not everywhere yet. We need to become rapid learners through connectivity, openness, discipline, collaboration, and a sense of curiosity. Organizations such as the Institute for Healthcare Improvement, Alliance for Community Health Plans, American Medical Group Association, American Medical Association, and Department of Defense are fostering connections among health care organizations as well as other health care stakeholders, and their efforts are gaining momentum.

I need to share a story of a physician who took on a leadership role based on his own dedication and determination when there was little or no interest in the changes that he believed needed to be completed. This is a story about the first physician at Kaiser Permanente, a visionary named Dr. Sidney Garfield.

In 1933, Dr. Garfield opened the Contractors General Hospital in the Mojave Desert to care for five thousand people who were working on the Colorado River Aqueduct project. The insurance companies were slow to pay, so Dr. Garfield made an agreement with them for prepayment at a nickel a day, per worker. Ninety-five percent of the workers signed up, and the hospital provided medical and hospital care for workers injured by industrial accidents. For an additional nickel a day, he offered total care, including non-work-related care for a dime a day.

Dr. Garfield was a person with clear values, energy, and a relentless focus to tackle problems he was seeing in large numbers of workers who had little health care and nothing resembling preventive care. He pondered the needs of these hardworking people and was determined to find an answer while it was painfully clear that there was no solution in place. His personal success traits that enabled him to find solutions that truly did not exist at the time were: pragmatism, idealism, and activism. As a pragmatist, he looked at the reality he was facing with totally objective eyes and no sugarcoating. Dr. Garfield believed the system wasn't working for the working man, or for the poor, and he didn't like that. As an idealist, he didn't believe that health care should just be a little better for all people, but that it should be available, high quality, affordable, and include prevention, which was not the norm at the time.

Dr. Garfield was also an activist. He thought people deserved great health care, but he didn't think he should sit around and wait for somebody else to do something about that. Instead, Dr. Garfield rolled up his sleeves. Pragmatist, idealist, and activist: he embodied all those traits and utilized them to affect profound change in health care. Dr. Garfield was essentially the first Permanente physician who partnered with Henry Kaiser to form Kaiser Permanente, a prepaid partnership between health insurance and physicians. This was unheard of at the time, criticized by organized medicine, and many viewed the move as quite radical.

We can choose to care, and then choose to act. We can choose to be a little more like Dr. Sidney Garfield. How you manage yourself is the first step to taking on these roles.

MY BACKGROUND

While this book isn't autobiographical, some information here about my professional career is needed to provide context for the coming chapters. Indulge me for a few paragraphs.

When I began medical school, I didn't have a clear sense of what I wanted to do as a physician. The only doctors I knew were family doctors—so I thought I'd probably have a family practice like one of them. But while in medical school, I discovered that I liked surgery and pediatrics, so I looked for a field where I could work in both disciplines. That led me to plastic surgery, but not only the cosmetic type of surgery. I was drawn instead to surgery that, when done properly, could make a radical difference for children who were born with or had incurred a deformity. I went into private practice in Denver, Colorado, with two seasoned and highly respected plastic surgeons, and the practice flourished.

At about this time, insurance companies began to increase their influence in health care, and not for the better. They started a system called "managed care," where insurance companies used their leverage to try and manipulate doctors and patients by controlling more clinical care and decision-making. Many of us believed they were trying to save money, and while that may or may not be true, it was how many disgruntled doctors interpreted the move toward managed care.

At this time, Kaiser Permanente in Denver had a physician-led medical group, and from what I observed, they appeared to be a very high-quality organization with physician leaders, a role that was new to me at the time. I really liked the fact that their clinical leaders had a strong and equal voice with the insurance entity, so I decided to join Kaiser Permanente, and in 1990, I started their plastic surgery program.

Because of the pressures exerted by the "managed care" movement and companies, Kaiser Permanente found itself having to compete with them. This tension of staying true to our values and competing was tough, and we had some challenging times.

At that time, there was a lot of turmoil in medicine, including internally at Kaiser Permanente. People were upset and some of them were leaving. I was recruited to run for the board of directors. They were looking for some leadership to represent them—the physicians—and so I was recruited because I believe they saw me as a respected clinician and not a firebrand, so I would listen with a balance of strength and compassion, but not too much emotion.

Two years after joining the board, I was elected president. There were financial issues and membership issues, but mostly, we were suffering from a morale vortex. Good doctors were leaving to go to other practices, and we had to create and maintain a better environment if we wanted to keep these people on.

My priorities, while I was the president of the medical group in Colorado, were: (1) preservation and enhancement of career; (2) optimizing the care experience, which required better access to services; and (3) streamlining their process to improve efficiency and effectiveness.

My priority, the notion of paying attention to careers, was not widely accepted by all the business leaders in the organization. They thought I was extremely inexperienced. Who was I to believe I could protect the careers of doctors when times were so tough? Keep in mind that I never used the word "protect" and never saw my role as a protector of doctors, but I did want to improve their environment, and mostly, I wanted to hear what they had to say. I put together a team to help me out with this, a team with a strong human resources foundation, and we paid attention to these doctors' careers, and saw major improvements. The Colorado Region of Kaiser Permanente was already noted for quality of care, and innovation as grounding for restoring performance broadly.

PRESERVATION AND ENHANCEMENT OF CAREER

When I became president of our medical group in 1999, I wanted to understand why so many physicians seemed so unhappy. I was concerned for our future ability to push for performance improvements in addressing a number of business challenges, which could only happen with strong and enthusiastic physician engagement. I knew they were extremely well-trained and accustomed to working hard and being responsible for the well-being of their patients.

After I had spent several weeks meeting with them in small groups and listening to them, it was clear that their unhappiness was caused by frustration, as they felt most of the changes in health care and the health care environment were being made to them and not by them.

I determined that this amazing asset called the physician professional career needed attention or we would never get where we aspired to be. I carefully chose the words "Preservation and Enhancement of Career" to define an approach for the profession's ideals and need to study the issues and opportunities to make the profession more fulfilling for physicians and positive for patients. Critics challenged that my intent was to protect physicians from accountability for the problems in the business performance. However, it was quite the opposite. Enhancing physicians' sense of accountability supported a delivery of care that was best for patients.

Our leadership and board invested in learning and improving the experience of patients and the team, and we learned a lot about optimizing the function of teams that support each other and ways to improve appointments, care flow, and use of the EHR in positive ways. We tracked improvement with physician surveys and saw consistent improvement.

An awareness emerged of the seriousness of physician burnout. Over the past decade, this has received very encouraging attention from some very influential leaders.[11]

I believe we will gain the greatest understanding by approaching this problem of burnout and frustration with the same scientific rigor we deploy with all issues in clinical care. We need to clearly define the problem, research the state of knowledge, develop hypotheses to test, run a variety of experimental interventions to measure the results, and continue to devote ourselves to this endeavor, learning broadly as a learning coalition.

Is this patient-centered? I believe it is. We owe it to patients to ensure they are cared for by competent, caring, and enthusiastic physicians and teams.

The approach must be scientifically rigorous and avoid the two extremes of prejudgment. One is, "Oh, the poor doctors. I feel so bad for them." That is simplistic and could lead to empathy as our only result. The other is, "Nuts to them! They have a wonderful job, enormous respect, and make good money. They need to get over it." This is very dangerous as it overlooks the seriousness of the issues confronting these well-trained and hurting professionals.

If we can apply the wonders of our science to medical conditions, we can apply some of the same rigor and effort to this major problem.

I was the physician leader of the Colorado region of Kaiser Permanente from 1999 to 2007. During that time, the region experienced vast improvements through the efforts of my team and many others from the medical group and health plan. In 2007, I was recruited to take on a national physician leadership role. That year, I accepted the position of executive director of the Permanente Federation, which is the national organizational component of the eight Permanente medical groups.

That's where my desire to instill a learning culture began. This arose from asking many questions, such as, "Why does one region have the best results for treating diabetes, while another is well behind yet excels at treating lung cancer?" There were incredible learning environments waiting to be explored and exploited for the benefit of the physician and the patient. I continued to understand the importance of continuous learning in the medical community, and that is what drove me to make learning a key area in developing physicians and their cultural environment. We could learn individually, as teams, and across regions. There was so much opportunity at our fingertips, and the results were very gratifying.

While I was in that position, I coauthored *The Doctor Crisis: How Physicians Can, and Must, Lead the Way to*

11   Paul Grundy, Kay R. Hagan, Jennie Chin Hansen, and Kevin Grumbach, "The Multi-Stakeholder Movement for Primary Care Renewal and Reform," *Health Affairs* 29, no. 5 (May 2010), accessed February 1, 2018, https://www.healthaffairs.org/doi/abs/10.1377/hlthaff.2010.0084; Amireh Ghorob and Thomas Bodenheimer, "Sharing the Care to Improve Access to Primary Care," *The New England Journal of Medicine* (May 24, 2012) 1955-1957; Thomas Bodenheimer, Amireh Ghorob, Rachel Willard-Grace, and Kevin Grumbach, "The Ten Building Blocks of High-Performing Primary Care, *Annals of Family Medicine* 12, no. 2 (March–April 2013): 166-171; and Christine A. Sinsky, Rachel Willard-Grace, Andrew M. Schutzbank, Thomas A. Sinsky, David Margolius, and Thomas Bodenheimer, "In Search of Joy in Practice: A Report of 23 High-Functioning Primary Care Practices," *Annals of Family Medicine* 11, no. 3 (May–June 2013): 272-278.

Better Health Care, published in 2014. While *The Doctor Crisis* was a narrative about my experiences and lessons learned as a clinician and then as a leader in the health field, I was often asked why I didn't put all my learning into a manual of sorts. I was involved with leadership training, and my students told me they enjoyed my lectures, slides, and handouts, but they needed more. They wanted a book that they could refer to, a manual of what I was teaching in the classroom.

Drawing on my experiences and knowledge, and with a distinct eye for what my physician audience—you, the reader—already knows, wants to know, and needs to know, I have done my best to do just that: create a manual for you to follow in your own journey and development as physician healer, leader, and partner. This book includes lessons from my own learning, spanning nearly three decades as a practicing surgeon, hospital leader, medical group leader, and national CEO.

My wish for you is to learn from my experiences and adopt a broader view of your abilities, your impact, and even your legacy as they relate to what's possible when you embrace the roles of leader, healer, and partner.

CHAPTER 2

THE HEALER'S JOURNEY

❓ WICKED QUESTION

Is leadership innate or developed?

One of the most challenging issues with physicians who are trying to take on leadership roles is how they act and react to challenges, confrontation, and inconvenient situations. With the mantle of leadership must come the understanding that leadership is not a "part-time" commitment.

That's not how leadership works. As a physician and a leader, you are always a physician, but you are also a leader 24/7 and not only when it's convenient. On top of that, as a leader, it's not enough to be bright. It's not even enough to be right. You also must be effective. You can have the right thinking and come up with the right answer, but how you manage yourself—through deliberating, debating, and other exchanges—can lay waste to the best-laid plans. A key to success of being an effective leader is knowing how to manage yourself and learning to be effective when you encounter the inevitable, frequent, and regular feedback and pushback.

As physicians, prone to intellectual skepticism because our education is within rigorous science and proof is always expected, we must be conscious of how we wield that skepticism in our position as leader. How we manage ourselves in those situations is critical to what defines us. Leadership doesn't rely on being smarter, stronger, or having a higher rank than our peers. Leadership relies on our ability to be the kind of person who can work with strong, opinionated, challenging colleagues to lead change.

In many industries, moving into a position of leadership is considered a promotion. That's not necessarily the case in medicine. First, that change in position requires you to give up your status as a full-time physician, which can affect your credibility. And if you weren't a very good physician before you moved to a leadership position, don't expect a free pass. Rather, you will face an uphill battle. If you don't bring that credibility with you as a clinical physician, it will not automatically be granted to you along with the new title.

However, even if you are a good clinician, that status doesn't automatically carry over into your new role either. People who respect you as a doctor may not automatically offer the same respect to you as their leader. Your clinical credibility gives you a voice, and people will be more willing to listen to what you have to say, but you can't rely on that forever and, instead, must learn your new craft, which is leading your team and the organization.

Often, physicians begin from a place of deficit when they take on a full-time leadership position because they're seen as having gone to the dark side of administration. When a business leader moves into a VP role, they're given a lot of credibility because they've made a transition. However, when a physician moves to a VP role, they not only have to learn the craft but also have to re-create and reestablish credibility.

If you go back and read those paragraphs you wrote on your medical school application, you'll find them teeming with idealism and a desire to serve and to heal. Those reasons are universal among medical school hopefuls. And yet, we now find doctors who—years later, when they've been practicing for decades—have begun to feel unhappy, disillusioned, and frustrated. I have observed that the core issue is less that physicians are overworked, and more that they are over-frustrated. What happened to that idealist? Why is it that some people can maintain or reboot their personal sense of mission while others do not and cannot? Why do so many physicians allow the disappointments, and the changes around them in the medical field, to strip them of their enthusiasm and their zeal to serve, to heal? When did they check out and why? The leverage of enthusiasm of physicians for their profession and the resulting positive impact on patients is why preservation and enhancement of career must continue to be the focus, and we must find meaningful ways to improve the professional experience.

Something happens to physicians amid all the years of study and learning medically and scientifically complex clinical subjects and the long hours at work, giving care. They strive for excellence, and they want to do the right thing, believing this profession will provide a good life for them, a meaningful life. But somewhere along the road, many physicians grow increasingly frustrated by the changes to their world and the belief that these changes are happening around them and being done to them—not caused by them and not within their control.

So, who's to blame for the slow chipping away of our beliefs in the profession, of our idealism? For many of us, there's a tendency to sit on the sidelines and blame everyone else: pharmaceutical companies, trial lawyers, hospitals, insurance companies, and patients. There are many actors in health care, and we believe they can and should all do better. However, eighty-three cents of every health care dollar is spent on health care delivery, and the decision of how that eighty-three cents is spent is generally made jointly by doctors and patients. Those other people and entities—pharmaceutical companies, lawyers, hospitals, insurance companies—have input and influence, but the physician and patient remain at the center of the critical decisions. As physicians, we have a majority of the control in how care is delivered. We can still have opinions on all the other players, and we can play a role in confronting the issues and challenges they present, but that doesn't change the fact that we wield tremendous influence over a significant percentage of how health care dollars are spent and how care is delivered.

🔑 KEY POINT

We need to run out of people to blame.

Medical school rewards academic prowess and, while knowledge is important, it is not the key to leadership. That distinction highlights a crucial difference between the good doctor and the good leader. Even an MBA degree, while it bestows upon the learner a lot of knowledge, does not ensure great leadership but rather reinforces the idea that leadership may be conferred purely via academics. An MD and an MBA may make you a better medical person or business person respectively, but neither ensures you will be a successful leader.

Leadership doesn't depend on a degree and it doesn't rely on promotions either. A physician may get promoted to chairman, chief, dean, or president of a medical school, hospital, medical group, or health system. Those promotions are often based on intellectual and academic prowess and performance, which may or may not correlate with leadership ability.

Some doctors will tell you they didn't get into this profession to even have the conversation about leadership. They don't think the role is applicable to what they do or is attainable for them. Their attitude is, "I can't do it and I don't want to do it. I'm a good doctor. I signed up to work hard in premed, get into a good medical school, make good grades, and get into a residency so I could work one hundred hours a week, then pass my boards and go into a practice where I take calls—often in the middle of the night—and deliver great care to my patients. That's what I signed up for, so please don't talk to me about leadership."

THE ROLE OF PATIENT

Patients don't want to be patients. The role of patient is involuntary and often instantaneous. Some might question that statement with the response, "Wait a second, I know patients who are obese and who don't exercise or follow a healthy diet. Aren't they contributing to their health problems?" Of course, I understand that and am not debating that reality. People do need to be responsible for those factors that contribute to their health and that are within their own control, and they need to be accountable to themselves. But we must always remember that the doctor-patient relationship works best when both assume their share of responsibility and collaborate toward the optimal outcome. Given all these factors, what, then, is the role of the patient?

> ## 🔑 KEY POINT
>
> The role of the patient is involuntary and often instantaneous.

Patients develop a wide variety of problems, conditions, and diseases, and the causes of these problems also vary widely. Society and even the health professions don't always treat these widely variable conditions with the same depth of understanding, empathy, and attention. We often naturally decide that someone with cancer or heart disease or a congenital deformity is an innocent victim of their medical condition. And yet we find other conditions less worthy of the same depth of understanding and empathy. But suffering is blind. Suffering does not know what causes it; it just is. And to the patient, it's painful, regardless of the cause. This tendency to judge extends beyond the typical maladies to other issues such as learning disabilities, gender identification, and psychological behavioral problems. We don't get to decide which diseases are worth our sympathy and worthy of our love and care. They all affect people, and it is the people—the patients—who need our focus and our services.

> ### ⚡ VOLTAGE DROP
>
> Because suffering is blind, physicians' opinions, words, and actions are carefully observed and heard. If we openly declare and model that some suffering is worth our empathy and understanding but others aren't, the message is heard, and echoes.

Consider the rate of suicide among women with breast cancer versus that of women seeking gender reassignment to become male. One of them is very high. Can you guess which one? Is it because they're bad people, or is the higher suicide rate because suffering is blind and can be quelled to a degree with our nonjudgmental application of sympathy and care?

SUFFERING IS BLIND

While the issue of suffering is not the focus of this book, the subject deserves attention from the medical community. When I was a full-time surgeon, if I was doing reconstruction surgery on a mastectomy patient, the mood of the operating room—and the attitude of the staff and the patient's family—would be one of undeniable support. If, on that same day, I saw a patient who had a man's body and was seeking surgery to help them become a woman, the tone might shift to one varying from avoidance to even judgment. Sure, some of the staff and the family of the patient would be supportive, but some would not. This isn't a rare response—it happens every day and is, unfortunately, too common.

My specialty, plastic surgery, has renamed the procedures around gender reassignment, adopting the term "gender repair." They have embraced the opinion that they are fixing something that wasn't quite right to begin with and, with this new terminology, casting those procedures in a kinder, more positive and caring light. This is an encouraging turn for the health care community and, indeed, for the patient whose suffering deserves our unbiased service.

The physician's role here, and how the physician manages themselves, is how they set the tone for their medical team. A doctor who takes the stance that all suffering is blind and who sets that tone in the medical office and in the operating room can have a tremendous impact on how the patient is received and cared for by the medical team.

Some physicians believe the financial issues around health care, the affordability and the access, are not their problem. I disagree. If the decisions we make cost people money—and they do—then we should care about how they affect our patients financially. When it comes to serving our patients, we can't opt in and out of the broader problems beyond medical treatments that affect our patients due to their participation in the health care industry. That may be a battle with the insurance companies and pharmaceutical corporations, but if that battle is not ours, then whose is it? We need to stand up for our patients on that front as well. It's not easy, but we can have an impact. Change—positive change—can happen if we choose to be involved.

Let's not forget that eighty-three cents of every health care dollar is spent on health care delivery, and that we, as doctors, have a heavy hand in how that money is spent. We want to spend it on the highest quality care, based on the best science.

HEALTH CARE HAS CHANGED

Health care has changed over the years, moving from simple, to complicated, to complex. For example, a simple problem might be an infectious disease such as strep throat or a urinary tract infection. A patient saw their doctor, who confirmed the symptoms and maybe took a culture, and there was a treatment. Simple health problems had relatively clear definitions and were finite conditions, and proven interventions provided simple solutions. We didn't have the diagnostic information or capabilities that we have today, and health care was simple.

Patients also develop more complicated conditions such as heart disease, cancer, and dysfunctions of other organ systems. These conditions were researched deeply, and many great advances were discovered. But as we gained more information and capability around complicated diseases, we developed cures for them. However, along with the cures came greater longevity, and so now a survivor of one complicated disease might develop more serious, and often chronic, conditions. More and better information, diagnostic capabilities, and cures, have increased life expectancy but in turn have created more complicated medical issues. These issues can't be solved by simple solutions; they require some coordination and orchestration. There is learning involved, more thought, and more flexibility in devising the solution.

A surgery is one example of a complicated solution. Although there is much information from a variety of inputs, it is the surgeon's duty to gather and leverage that information to ensure the right diagnosis is reached. Then, the surgeon must select the right venue for the surgery, which could be a hospital or a day-use facility and assemble the right team. There are other considerations, such as anesthesia, labs, the right equipment, and even the right type of sutures. Many variables contribute to this complicated solution and they must be communicated to the patient. The patient needs to prepare for these variables and the solution.

We can solve simple and complicated problems, but additional changes evolved that created complex problems which cannot be solved by the same skillsets we used for solving simple and complicated problems. What differentiates the complicated from the complex? While a complicated issue can be solved by a linear solution, complex issues cannot because several processes—often driven by several experts—may be running in parallel, or perhaps in conflict, toward the solution. These various experts or constituencies have developed deep expertise in their own areas of complicated science. The newer challenge inherent in complexity is that there is no linear solution that can be provided and overseen by one expert or from one discipline. To solve these complex problems, these diverse experts and participants, the decision-makers, need to work together and, through collaboration, cooperation, and group effort and learning, develop complex solutions.

In a complicated system, someone can be in charge; in a complex system, many stakeholders and influencers with different knowledge and often conflicting interests and needs exist. No one person or entity has the knowledge or the power to determine or enforce the best solution to a complex problem.

LINEAR SOLUTIONS DON'T SOLVE COMPLEX ISSUES: THE POLITICAL RAMIFICATIONS

Solving complicated problems in medicine requires someone to consider and combine many variables into a linear solution. That someone is usually the physician or surgeon who is skilled at their specialty but also skilled at organizing, orchestrating, aligning, and executing to accomplish a goal and solve a problem. Complicated problems arise all the time around the world. That is the world President Trump came from. To put up a high-rise in Abu Dhabi, for example, a person must work with the government, get permits, acquire land, deal with the unions, and figure out the water, utilities, and all the other parts and pieces that go into building a high-rise. There's a lot of input, and it's complicated, but it's also relatively linear because one person—the person in charge—can make most of the decisions. In that world, Trump was successful.

However, he's now in a complex world, and it is very different. Nowhere is this more evident than in his dealings with foreign policy and health care. He will never get anything meaningful accomplished on either front by putting people behind closed doors and telling them what he demands. And like other world problems of the recent past, we can no longer solve health care policy issues with a bigger, stronger, all-powerful leader telling us what to do. The requirements of inclusion of various constituent views and the ability to convene these various strong experts to pursue a process of building shared context, debate the implications of difference, and make a disciplined commitment to a shared successful solution are essential. And because no single person or constituency has enough knowledge, power, or influence to get their way, the process of debate, learning, challenging, and compromising is the path that must be taken. Too many of the participants are trying to rely on the power and influence they enjoyed in their world of complicated problems, and they will never get the best results for as many as possible.

Health care is like this—a complex, adaptive system. Health care systems revolve around leaders who work together, collaborate, and compromise to solve problems. No one person in that system has the authority, information, money, knowledge, or force to tell everyone else what to do. The doctors don't have that authority, pharmaceutical companies don't, insurance companies don't, and the hospitals don't have it either. Each entity has its own agenda and issues, but they all work together to provide solutions to health care issues. That is why an individual representing any of those entities must be a different kind of leader—the kind who understands complex, adaptive systems. In these systems, you can own part of a solution where everyone is in complete agreement, but on another part of the issue, everyone's solution can vary dramatically, and in fact, you may find yourself opposite from another decision-maker who you were beginning to view as your ally. That doesn't make either one of you right or wrong; you simply are seeing that part of the issue from a different perspective, so your solutions will differ. The key point here is that while governing by power and force in a linear fashion may work on some issues, it does not work well on the complex issue of health care policy.

This increasing complexity of knowledge, technology, information, and even patients cannot be solved by linear solutions but requires integration and coordination from multiple sources and a rich level of cooperation and relationships, all supported by easily accessible information. It demands the accelerated development of Information Age solutions—information-rich solutions that leverage information, technology, analytics, associated tools, and teams focused on the needs of patients as individuals and partners in their own care.

These changes, which, for many of us, have taken place within our careers as physicians, have created an environment where we may be stuck in the Industrial Age of medicine, which depended on the doctor-patient visit. During that age, the doctor saw you and diagnosed you with his own eyes, ears, brain, and perhaps a limited number of tests. Physicians provided a treatment, and the patient paid them—it was very transactional. Another important distinction of the Industrial Age was that the doctor had the knowledge and the power.

The shift from Industrial to Information Age isn't unique to the medical field. In the last age, the Industrial Age, businesses had the knowledge and the power, but today, consumers can get information and make purchases online. They have access to expertise and can make transactions from their mobile devices. That is a huge shift of power, in business and in medicine, and the medical world has been slow to adapt.

Physicians need to move quickly into the Information Age. We, as physicians, need to meet this new age head-on as problem-solvers equipped to lead in a world of complex, adaptive systems. In this Information Age, we must partner with patients, the primary care team, the information technology team, and with other physicians and specialists. Like the hub of a wheel with many spokes, we must adapt and be able to gather, analyze, and interpret the data for our patients daily. For a doctor who's in his fifties or sixties and who's used to everything revolving around the office visit, that is a big ask. For any physician, it's a lot to ask, and it begins with how we choose to manage ourselves as leaders.

CHAPTER 3

THE CRUX

❓ WICKED QUESTION

What is your fundamental belief and bias toward your fellow man?

Everyone in health care has plenty of thoughtful ideas for how to improve health care. They all seem to feel there's a lot of potential, but they also seem to share the same barrier.

The questions I get asked most often start with the same six words: How do you get doctors to...?

- How do you get doctors to measure quality?
- How do you get doctors to understand that affordability is part of their responsibility?
- How do you get doctors to be nicer to nurses?

- How do you get doctors to discipline their peers?

There's a whole litany of questions, all starting with those six little words: How do you get doctors to...?

The bigger and perhaps all-encompassing question might be: How do you get doctors to be broad owners on the issues of health care? Because again, a person in the position of leadership doesn't opt out of issues that affect the patient. The leader says, "If it's affecting the patient, I will at least listen and see if I can contribute to a solution." But we have no leadership training, and that's part of the problem. Most of our training is around taking individual tests and written or oral exams. These aren't team tests, and we are never given any kind of training on how to work together as a team, process information as a group, or collaborate with others.

As basic to accomplished leaders as some leadership skills are, most of these techniques—setting standards, counseling, encouraging, teamwork, rewarding performance and challenging one's own organization—are typically not discussed in formal medical school training.

—MARK HERTLING

We want and need doctors to step up, but the challenge remains that many do not want to, and those who do haven't had the training. They know that change needs to occur for improvement to take place, and they are willing to drive that change, but how? Those physicians are stuck in the middle of the dilemma, wanting to help but not knowing where to start. My goal then with this book is to assist any physician ready and willing to take that next step.

Those who are willing to take on the role of healer, leader, and partner need to embrace the idea that health care is about the patient's experience. The medical industry has evolved from doctor- to patient-centered, and your belief system is where leadership begins. That is the crux of becoming a leader, and your starting point. Pause and ask yourself what you believe. What do you believe about yourself and your role as physician? What do you believe about your fellow man? Are your beliefs positive or negative? You must understand that completely to become the leader you need to be. That is the crux.

YOUR BELIEF SYSTEM IS PIVOTAL

Each of us has a set of values at our core that permeates our relationships and interactions as leaders. Basically, these values answer the question, "What do you believe about other people?" Do you believe they're trustworthy and have good intentions? Or do you believe they're self-centered and not to be trusted? Understand that about yourself—your basic beliefs about other people—because if you approach the world with a negative filter, it will influence your approach to leadership. You may not even be aware that you have an overlying filter, but if you don't acknowledge it and deal with it, you may not be able to affect the positive changes you desire and won't even know why.

Now, seeing the world through either filter—the positive or the negative—and following its respective path can lead to organizational successes. And while these differing views toward our fellow colleagues are not 100 percent absolute, they are very useful constructs to frame this discussion. Even an extremely negative approach can bring about profitability and other positive results. However, the path you take creates very different cultures.

Every man must decide whether he will walk in the light of creative altruism or in the darkness of destructive selfishness.

—MARTIN LUTHER KING

Thomas Hobbes and Thomas Locke were seventeenth-century English philosophers who held these contrasting views of the nature of people and the role of government. Hobbes believed people were wicked and selfish and always acted in their own best interests and were best governed by an absolute monarch. Locke believed that people were by nature good and would learn from their experiences. He believed that with the right information, people could be trusted to make the right decisions and govern themselves: democracy!

Ask yourself whether you would prefer to work at the organization where leaders, coworkers, and patients view physicians with distrust or one where they assume others' intentions are trusted and positive. Which organization and leadership style would you submit your family members to, if they were entering the medical profession?

Our personal bias informs our style and behavior, which has a major influence on the culture that is created in our organization. While we have noted that a low trust and coercive leadership style can deliver business success measured by finances, growth, and product acceptance, the resultant culture is not ideal, especially in health care. Dr. Lucian Leape, an early researcher on safety in health care, while testifying at the US Congress House Committee on Veteran's Affairs, briefed the committee on the state of human error management in the US medical industry. Leape made multiple important points illuminating the extensive cultural issues in health care, but his most demanding comment was, "we punish people for making mistakes."[1]

---

1   Lucian Leape, US Congress House Committee on Veteran's Affairs Testimony, October 12,1997.

Major inconsistencies in leaders' behaviors are undermining. When a leader declares openly and widely that they support and demand an open, accepting, psychologically safe environment, it sends a positive signal. When that same leader then messages his closest senior leaders that they need to do the tough work of delivering the numbers as the true measure of their success, it creates a subculture that rolls its eyes at the public declarations because the real rules are "make the numbers."

Dr. Amy Edmondson, a professor at the Harvard Business School, is a leader in researching and understanding the issues and impact of psychological safety in the workplace. Her research is widely respected, but she has some special learnings that apply to health care. Edmondson clarifies the differences between interpersonal trust and psychological safety by framing "trust as an expectation that others' future actions will be favorable to one's interest; psychological safety refers to a climate in which people are comfortable being and expressing themselves."[2] As the patient- and employee-safety body of knowledge evolves, the implications for psychological safety of the team become increasingly clear for patient safety. There are many factors essential for a culture to be psychologically safe and important aspects of leader-

---

2   Amy C. Edmondson, "Psychological Safety, Trust and Learning: A Group-Level Lens," in *Trust and Distrust in Organizations: Dilemmas and Approaches*, edited by Roderick Kramer and Karen Cook (New York: Russell Sage Foundation, 2004), 239-272.

ship behavior include: accessibility and availability, being open to and inviting input, and modelling curiosity and fallibility. Professor Edmondson also differentiates the traditional concept of teams which can imply a static structure, with the idea of "teaming," which is an evolved cultural competency that is flexible, mobile, and adaptable to real time situations.[3] We initially noted that both extremes of the crux of leadership can create business success; however, these organizations will fall short when success is assessed more broadly.

The progress of psychological safety is clear in health care championed by organizations like AHRQ, IHI, NCQA, JCAHO, Leapfrog, etc., but the progressive understanding and endorsement more broadly are illustrated by Google's declaration that of the five most important traits of their successful teams, number one is psychological safety.[4]

EXAMINE YOUR CORE

At its core, the crux of leadership follows one of two mindsets. The first mindset is one of low trust and low expectation, as seen in a person who leads with force or

---

3   Amy C. Edmondson, *Teaming: How Organizations Learn, Innovate, and Compete in the Knowledge Economy* (San Francisco: Jossey-Bass, 2012).

4   Shana Lebowitz, "Google Considers This to Be the Most Critical Trait of Successful Teams," *Business Insider*, November 20, 2015, accessed February 1, 2018, http://www.businessinsider.com/amy-edmondson-on-psychological-safety-2015-11.

by fooling people with manipulation or ultimatums. This mindset promotes a culture of low psychological safety. The second mindset is one of high trust and expectation, where a leader listens, acknowledges, challenges, learns, and cocreates shared context and solutions, promoting a culture of high psychological safety.

These two mindsets are self-fulfilling. If you truly believe your coworkers, peers, and all the other players in health care are just in it for themselves, and you expect them to view ideas for improvement with a self-centered lens, you will probably not be disappointed. If you think the people in one of your clinical departments are a bunch of jerks and their tendency is to do what is best for them without concern for other team members or even the patient, you will inevitably adopt an attitude wrapped in cynicism. Your leadership style will reflect this attitude, as you rely on techniques such as manipulation, coercion, and threats to either fool people or force them to go along with you. There are so-called leaders who follow this way of thinking without being aware of it, perhaps because they had a leadership training course or read a book and know just enough about the subject to have convinced themselves they're experts. Yet they are still cynical. A physician who, in earnest, is striving to develop his leadership skills might engage in conversation with an "expert" such as this only to be shut down with a clever quip—something they learned and have been waiting for that just-right time to throw out there rather than listening and working to be part of the solution. I remember trying to make a point to a leader who didn't value feedback very much, and when he tired of me, he said, "Well, it looks like somebody moved your cheese!" That was not an impactful reply, and comments like that can be demeaning, but you must choose the high road in those instances and not become a victim of the very culture and mindset you are seeking to avoid.

A better way to approach your fellow man is, of course, with an open heart. If you believe that most people want to do the right thing, you will lead accordingly. Of course, doing the right thing requires the right information and capabilities, both of which are important. Of course, there's nothing absolute, and every organization has its jerks, people who are in it for themselves and have no interest at all in working together toward positive solutions. However, if your general belief is that most people are good, you will trust them, listen to them, and be open to exploring your differences. Building trust is slow at first, but over time, you will build momentum, and the trust will come more quickly. You can get there by following a process of listening and acknowledging, along with respectful debate. You must listen to the information provided, compare it to your own data and information, and seek to identify the commonalities and to question the differences. The process requires patience and persistence, and the first time will seem sluggish and incredibly, painfully slow. But that's how you build the trusting relationship, and in time, momentum and solutions will come more quickly and be much easier to reach.

Having an open heart and believing the best about others does not imply naïveté. While we must believe in the positives, we must also be realists, willing to argue with knowledge and techniques to deal with the inevitable difficulty and negatives.

We'll talk more about the role of communication as it relates to effective leadership in chapter 4, "Communication," and the role of self-awareness in motivational and management styles in chapter 5, "Develop Great Leaders and Teams."

🔑 KEY POINT

Leadership in One Sentence

Effective leadership is a continuous process of sharing context and information, listening, challenging, and persisting in this iterative process to develop shared context and mutual learning, and cocreate understanding and solutions.

CHAPTER 4

COMMUNICATION

❓ WICKED QUESTION

Why do some intelligent and rational people not get it?

Your role as a physician and leader requires exceptional communication skills. How you communicate with people—especially those who disagree with you, question you, or call BS on your ideas—shows everyone what kind of leader you are.

As a presenter, you must be open to disagreement and questions. At some point, you'll be face-to-face with thirty-five people, and three of them will try to make that time miserable, asking you tough, sometimes unfair, questions. How you manage yourself and react says a lot to the other thirty-two people in the room. They might be thinking, "I like this person and how they handled themselves with these hostile colleagues. I think this person's a good leader. I don't want these other guys to continue dominating this conversation."

> ### 🔑 KEY POINT
>
> Anyone can show slides to silent people. Leaders earn their stripes in Q&A.

Whether your content is excellent or not, the challenges to the speaker often accelerate in Q&A. It is important for the speaker to understand that while they did their best to provide credible content in an effective way, the reaction of the audience can be influenced not only by the content and presentation, but also by their own frame of reference. Their reaction may be influenced by their own knowledge, preexisting bias, or frank misunderstanding of your presentation.

Peers are equals. They're bright and thoughtful. If you present your ideas to them, they should question and debate you when necessary to help you improve. However, challenging questions can be little kernels that allow for greater learning and growth. You lose their respect if you are dismissive or demeaning of the question or the individual rather than objectively acknowledging their point and providing the most informed answer you can.

Leadership *is* communication. It's a continuous process of listening, sharing context, and learning. As the CEO or chief, I might have information you will not like, but I must share my knowledge with you, as you must share yours with me. Often, we can't solve my problem without solving yours, so we must make a conscious effort to communicate with one another.

Communication revolves around the relationship you build with your team, the organization, and your direct reports. Invest in the process of communication by listening, sharing context, gaining different perspectives, challenging one another, and having this two-way, back-and-forth continuous process. Communication isn't just something that a leader does. It's a way of being with the people in your organization.

HOW TO TALK TO PATIENTS IN THE INFORMATION AGE

Health care is much more complicated these days, in part because people have access to more information. Patients have more knowledge about their illness, but they might have a lot of misinformation too.

Now more than ever, communication is as important in your role as healer as it is in your roles as leader and partner. Listen for verbal cues from your patient that more communication is needed. A patient's unreasonable demand often signals low trust due to insufficient information or lack of understanding. For example, a patient will say, "I twisted my knee and I need an MRI scan." If you ask them why they need an MRI scan, they tell you they want a thorough assessment of their injury. This is part of the American myth of health care, in which physicians are expected to do more tests and X-rays than what's required to prove we're competent, thorough, and concerned.

> ## 🔑 KEY POINT
>
> Unreasonable demand is often the patient's proxy for poor trust, access, or continuity.

Maximum intervention, such as an MRI, on the first indication of a symptom happens too frequently in the United States without solid evidence to support it. The best approach is to begin by listening carefully to the patient and asking clarifying questions to understand the history, and then do a thorough and careful exam. At this point, additional questions from both doctor and patient are pursued, and a plan is proposed. To assure the patient that the physician is competent, thorough, and concerned, it can be helpful to proactively mention options such as the MRI and where you see its role. Finally, an explanation of the treatment plan should be provided, along with a mention of possible modifications or adjustments that may be needed based on the response to the original therapy and progress or worsening in symptoms.

The challenge for doctors in the Information Age is how to not get defensive or bowled over by the amount of information patients have. A common frustration for physicians is figuring out how to cope with this complicated new world of self-monitoring devices, apps, and data. How does it fit in to the older health care model? To answer that question, we must ask some tough questions. How do we adopt some of those technologies in ways that allow patients to get better? Additionally, how do we adapt our role as a trusted confidant and healer to include these technologies? If patients relying on data from Watson, websites, blogs, patient groups, or other sources are a bother to you, you run the risk of not fulfilling your responsibility. This evolving new world will require that the role of the physician evolve as well.

CLEAR AND SUCCESSFUL COMMUNICATION

As a physician leader addressing a group, clear and successful communication starts with understanding your audience's level of understanding. I have three vital checkpoints for communication:

- What do they know?
- What do they want to know?

- What do they need to know?

Let's discuss each one.

WHAT DO THEY KNOW?

Recognize when a group has varying levels of information. Then, find a balance between talking beneath them, thus insulting them, and annoying them by talking over them. This is not always precise, but it's a good preparation exercise and can be quite valuable.

WHAT DO THEY WANT TO KNOW?

Try to understand your audience's frame of reference, why they are there and what matters to them. Their opinions and needs are based on their perspectives and points of view. Even if you don't agree with your audience, understanding them is key.

Once you understand their point of view, you shouldn't change your message to agree with it, but prepare yourself to either reinforce it or confront their reality by challenging it. This helps you connect with your audience.

Say you're a surgeon addressing a group of nurses. You'd tailor your message differently than you would for a group of surgeons, as the contrasting groups generally have different points of view. If you're talking about making a major change in the operating room, surgeons want to know how it affects the equipment and their schedule. However, the nurses might be concerned with how to rearrange the rooms to accommodate the patient positioning, instruments, and equipment. Their daily realities are different, so your presentation of information needs to be different.

WHAT DO THEY NEED TO KNOW?

Tailor your message to address what your audience wants to know and what you need them to know. Your depth of knowledge gives you many potential key teaching points that you could emphasize, but when you clearly know what they want to know, you can create a highly focused and impactful message match.

Rather than assume you know what people care about and want to learn more about, obtain clarification from people in the group before you address the entire audience. Set up a call ahead of time with someone in the group to get their pulse. Tell the person you're unsure of the perspective of the group and want to know what they're thinking. Find out if there are any hot buttons or potentially charged issues that might evoke an emotional response from the group. Having this information ahead of time allows you to address it and even splice some of your key messages into it.

FIGURE OUT YOUR TONE

Addressing an audience with unwelcome news is challenging, but whatever message you have, consider your tone and how it suits the people receiving it. Do you want to be encouraging and positive? Or do you want to be alarming? Do you want to be concerning? What is the context of the day? What is the message of the day? How do you match it with a tone that will be neither disingenuously positive nor falsely menacing?

Say you have good news to share, and you're feeling effusive and jolly. You arrive hoping to cheer them up, but they might not want to be cheered up. Maybe only some people received their bonuses. If that's the case, you might not want to talk about how the hospital is purchasing new, expensive equipment because no one will want to hear about it. They'll think you're a clueless jerk, unaware of the real problems they're dealing with.

Before you arrive, think about the audience's mood. If they're in a foul one, don't try to cajole them into being jolly. Until you get through some of their emotive messaging and thinking, it will be difficult to get to the content you need to share. This is another instance where it helps to do your homework. If you're traveling to another clinic or department, contact them before you arrive. You should have a trusted colleague to call, perhaps your chief or department head. You may have to call someone closer to the group, and it may be someone who doesn't like you, but that doesn't matter if they know what's going on, have a sense of neutrality, and are willing to speak with you. In addition to being prepared, your success will depend heavily on how you carry and manage yourself.

REHEARSE

We may believe we're fantastic presenters or may equally be very uncomfortable in front of a group, but we can all improve with practice, input, and critical feedback. When it comes to presentations, in addition to knowing your material and audience, rehearsals are also key. While your slides and content may be informative and impactful, it's beneficial to rehearse alone, with a colleague, and with a professionally trained performer. Videotape yourself as well so you can recognize what you like and don't like about your performance. Practice and rehearsal are not just for entertainers. Speaking to an audience is also a performance of sorts, and your delivery affects how your content is heard.

Take time to do a dry run. Know the kind of flow you'll have in your presentation, paying attention to details such as what you want to point to and where you want to walk. Give this a try with trusted colleagues who will give you frank feedback. This practice is too often overlooked because we believe our content alone is sufficient. In this process, also be attentive to the total time of your presentation and ensure it ends within the time you are allotted. The people who have put on the program and the audience have an expectation regarding the content that will be presented within a specific timeframe, so you should honor that expectation. If there are other presenters, do not infringe on their time. Like you, they, too, have committed considerable time and effort creating and practicing their presentations and deserve to be heard.

⚡ VOLTAGE DROP

Leaders who work hard to deliver high-impact speeches and presentations must also anticipate a range of possible questions after the presentation. These can range widely from simply requesting clarification, to challenging information or conclusions, all the way to highly personal attacks or provocations based on content or external context. When the speaker reacts personally by being demeaning of the individual or dismissive of the question, the voltage drop from the high impact of the presentation and content can be huge. Managing yourself to listen, acknowledge, challenge, and cocreate better understanding are essential to avoid losing traction from the core content.

THE CONTINUOUS ITERATIVE PROCESS

A Key Point from chapter 3 is relevant here as well, and bears repeating: "Effective leadership is a continuous process of sharing context and information, listening, challenging, and persisting in this iterative process to develop shared context and mutual learning, and cocreate understanding and solutions."

The continuous iterative process involves fostering an environment in which opinions and criticism are welcome, especially when dealing with complex problems. Leaders must be very clear about what they think, feel, learn, and believe, and they must communicate in a way that people can fully agree or disagree with them. Anyone can show slides to silent people. You lead, listen, share your context of information, acknowledge your peers' context, and challenge this new dataset of combined information.

Challenging involves listening to understand and seek relevant knowledge. For example, say a hospital group wants to send more people to the emergency room. They may have good reasons for doing so, and you must listen to that positive side of their knowledge. However, the hospital has closed their emergency room for sixty days. You must listen to the group's reasoning while coping with the reality of the closure.

As a leader, you must acknowledge the group's reasons and communicate to them that while you agree in principle, the fact remains that the emergency room is closed for sixty days.

That's a simplistic example where you cannot accommodate the group, despite their solid reasoning. You will also encounter situations where, when you get one another's information, you conclude that your own idea, reasoning, or conclusion is incorrect. The iterative process of going back and forth to listen to what the other person says in reaction to you and vice versa—that persistence—helps you develop a shared context. Once everyone has laid their data on the table, you can look at the problem with a more adequate dataset. Some problems take minutes and some hours, while others take several sessions. As you work through problems together, you have the potential to reach a mutual understanding and then, cocreate solutions. Working together allows us to improve the overall quality of data, and to learn to collaborate and witness its value.

This continuous iterative process evolves over time, particularly when you're in a leadership position. As you return to old problems, you'll find new data points and realize what you thought would work is ineffective. You're in a constant state of sharing data on ongoing problems. This habitual procedure will help you attack recent problems as both a leader and a team partner. After making mistakes and taking months with the first issue, the second will be easier to tackle. You and your team have learned to work together and trust one another, and trust is the lever for speed. As you develop trust, you spend less time doubting one another. People become more willing to share their issues without fear of repercussions. The more you trust one another, the more quickly you gain momentum, and thus, solve problems.

> ### 🔑 KEY POINT
>
> Full credibility comes from both the ability to influence and also a demonstrated willingness to be influenced.

As the boss, you can't just bark orders. You must respect each person's knowledge. Again, listen, acknowledge, share information, and cocreate solutions. When times are tough, leaders stray from this process. They feel as if they don't have time to sit and debate the topic at hand. That's a natural response, but it's important to remember that other people have valuable contributions to make. Your job is to convey the reality from your point of view, and their job is to do the same so you can create a solution that solves problems on all levels, not just from one vantage point. People who believe they are more results-oriented may think listening and acknowledging are a waste of time and may miss the next step, which is the challenge. Challenging a colleague, partner, group, or your team might entail saying, "OK, I hear your information. I get it. Let me add this data because even if you and I agree you're right, there's no automatic solution here." You simultaneously understand and challenge their point of view. Listening goes both ways, and so they must listen to you too.

Then, repeat. They return to you with more information, and you listen, acknowledge, and so on. If you watch this technique play out, you will see the tension come and go. Eventually you will witness a significant cocreation of knowledge and context that allows everyone to look at the issue with a common viewpoint. When everyone has the same dataset, you will ultimately look at the data from the same point of view. The results, then, are less biased, less emotional, richer, and more likely to succeed. Long-term execution of the continuous iterative process within a group leads to the development of a trusting, can-do culture.

We'll talk more about dealing with difficult crowds in chapter 7, "The Difficult Crowd," and about building an empowered culture in chapter 10, "Culture."

One caveat to the continuous iterative process is that when everyone has the same information, they will likely come to the same conclusion, but that does not guarantee a great outcome. It's not a magical formula for the perfect solution but a process of respecting people's points of view, honoring their input, and continuously sharing the reality from your point of view to reach the most informed conclusion effectively and efficiently. You are also developing a culture that is more likely to arrive at informed and effective solutions, but there are also opportunities to leverage being 'wrong' when you acknowledge the learning and improve to grow.

THE LEADER'S CHALLENGE

The leader's challenge is to blend each party's knowledge into working together to find a better solution. That's what we live every day if we're doing our job.

Sometimes you have to return to problems based on new datasets. You don't want to negatively surprise people with major changes you neglected to communicate. In fact, you need to communicate information ten times more than you think you do because people are busy, distracted, and relatively unconcerned with some of your issues in contrast to their daily front-of-mind reality. They have their own challenges to deal with too.

Continuous, iterative communication may, at times, seem slow, and the road can be variable and bumpy, but long-term success and speed come from building trust, not from going fast. People have come to me months after reaching a conclusion or agreeing to a solution to thank me for sticking to this process. Eventually, people notice that you improve as an organization or department with a leader who takes the time to communicate all the facts.

With all this in mind, don't give up on the process and push for a consensus. This is a common response from people who don't have the full armamentaria of leadership. They have their brains, their rank, and what they believe are good solutions. When people push back, these leaders resort to clichéd sentiments meant to inspire a strong work ethic, while in reality, these clichés mask the leader's unwillingness to go through the continuous iterative process.

For example, we had a leader who prided himself on driving improvement and pushing for results. He would find a solution but didn't always take the time to listen or debate it with others. One of his classic, clichéd lines was, "I just want to check in and see if you're all on board with this." This created quite a reaction because "on board" translated to, "Are you going to get in line and do things my way because you're still not doing everything I want you to do?" This language choice is demeaning and threatening. A person on his team might be afraid to say, "Yes, I'm on board," because it implied they agreed. However, there was no process for them to express their opinion.

This example confirms Amy Edmondson's teachings on the importance of psychological safety in teams.

Recall the crux. As a leader, when you first examine yourself, decide what you think of your fellow colleagues, how you approach challenges, and how your beliefs about others and your approach impact your communication. If you are a person who doesn't want to take the time to hear contrasting opinions, you push forward with an agenda that requires a fair amount of obedience and control. On the other hand, if you intrinsically trust your fellow colleagues—and thus, your workers—you enact that continuous iterative process while remaining results-oriented. You build a culture that enables you to establish momentum and create more speed. Notably, both methodologies can foster results. Fear-based, hierarchical cultures can turn out profits and decent products in many companies. It's not that you'll fail with this model, but you will promote a fear-based environment that negatively impacts your patients and colleagues and clearly does not create the conditions for you to be a strong healer, leader, or partner.

PART II

PHYSICIAN AS LEADER

Physicians have worked hard to become trusted clinicians and healers to be able to provide care and caring to patients. But patients encounter the health care system physically, socially, psychologically, and financially, and deserve trusted support in navigating these complex realities. Because physicians have a disproportionate impact, they need to opt in to accept these challenges with an unwavering awareness of this total reality. This sense of accountability requires a commitment of time as well as growth and development to embrace and master new skills. While honoring the role of healer, we must embrace and strengthen the mantle of leader.

CHAPTER 5

DEVELOP GREAT LEADERS AND TEAMS

❓ WICKED QUESTION

Is a leadership position a promotion for a doctor?

Leadership is both learned and innate.

What you have innately can create real leverage or tremendous barriers to what you develop. No one begins the leadership journey with all the tools they need; they start with deficiencies. Assess yourself. Manage yourself. Understand where you are regarding the crux, have the right attitude, and be flexible with your reactions based on your biases. Assess yourself first, and then assess your initial team using tools of human resources and self-evaluation.

The capability to assess yourself depends on a commitment and willingness to build self-awareness. In today's business world, self-awareness tends to be an undervalued trait, often shrugged off as a nice-to-have ability. However, this belief couldn't be further from the truth. Building self-awareness is one of the most critical leadership skills needed today, and for organizations of the future. Tasha Eurich, in her recent book *Insights*, states, "Senior leaders who lack self-awareness are 600 percent more likely to derail, which can cost companies a staggering $50 million per executive."[1] Only after building a solid foundation of self-awareness and working diligently to uncover and address leadership challenges can a leader begin the important work of assessing one's team. Modeling the way, in this respect, creates an environment that reinforces the need for leadership development and the core belief that we all need to start with ourselves first. There are many resources available to assist with this self-discovery and leadership development work. I've found several to be exceptionally valuable in my own development, which I'll highlight in this chapter.

---

1   Tasha Eurich, *Insight: Why We're Not as Self-Aware as We Think, and How Seeing Ourselves Clearly Helps Us Succeed at Work and in Life*, (New York: Crown, 2017), 12.

Your own sense of clinical competence deserves some reflection. If you choose to pursue a leadership career move because you were unsuccessful or not very good at clinical practice, it is a very long road. When individuals follow a leadership track because their clinical competence is lacking, they begin with a significant challenge. This matters because trust is key to managing colleagues, managing change, and making improvements. Clinical competence doesn't make you a good leader or business person, but it is an indicator of your capability as a clinician, your personal behavior and integrity, and your behaviors as a colleague. If people are not receptive to your skills, your values, your integrity, and how you practice in a clinical sense, managing or working as a business administrator will be a very large hurdle.

THE ROLE OF EMOTIONAL INTELLIGENCE IN GREAT LEADERS

In health care, we come from a world of IQ. We rely on it for our whole development as physicians and receive training in the world of individual measurement and accomplishments. In the context of great leaders, we need to continue to honor content expertise and excellence of knowledge, but we also need to emphasize the role of emotional intelligence in order to influence and inspire as leaders. Understanding the EQ, the *emotional* rather than intelligence quotient, awareness of learning, managing yourself, and developing people will make you a better leader.

EQ relies on self-awareness, which is vital to good leadership. Self-aware leaders are fiercely focused on the problems but humble and understanding of other people and issues.

Like emotional intelligence and the premise of the crux, McGregor's Theory X and Theory Y styles of motivation and management are also contingent on self-awareness. In the 1960s, the psychologist Douglas McGregor developed a theory to explain how leaders or managers believe one of two things.

Theory X leaders innately believe people are not motivated and must be controlled and manipulated to perform well. These leaders display an authoritarian style of leadership. By contrast, Theory Y leaders assume that people are good at their core and are motivated by kindness and want to have a positive impact. These leaders display a participatory style of leadership.

Those two kinds of people—basically, those who assume the best about people and those who assume the worst—conflict with each other in organizations. People in either camp aren't wearing jerseys; you don't know who thinks what. When you walk into a room of your peers, or a room you're presenting to, you don't know who's operating in the Theory X or the Theory Y camp.

Given this, leaders should understand that where they lie in that continuum is not something to be understated. People can easily claim to believe in the goodness of others, but that claim doesn't make it intrinsically true. Their actions could tell an utterly different story. Leaders who claim to have faith in their teams only to attempt to control them lose their credibility quickly. The leader models and sets the tone for which theory the organization operates under and, in so doing, sets the tone for the culture.

Think of leadership and culture as two sides of the same coin. If the leader believes in the goodness of people, that Theory Y approach trickles down throughout the team and its culture. However, if the leader follows the Theory X style of motivation and management, and believes the team isn't motivated to do well for their patients, the leader sets a different tone and creates a different kind of culture. It all goes back to the crux, which is based on solid evidence purporting that you must be aware of where you stand and make your beliefs about others an intentional and purposeful driver as they relate to your leadership approach.

Checking yourself from a self-aware perspective becomes more difficult the higher you are in the organization because you often receive less feedback. Due to the political nature of most organizations, people are less likely to give truly honest feedback such as, "Hey, you know, Jack, in our meeting you showed up pretty arrogant," or, "Did you know that you interrupted this woman three times and she left feeling devalued?"

As a self-aware leader, constructive feedback becomes especially desirable. Showing up is very important in this space because you not only have to be present physically but also show an awareness, humility, and an open listening style to avoid creating a vicious cycle of isolation. Unless someone is willing to have that courageous conversation and address your shortcomings, you will remain isolated.

You need a trusted cadre of people around you who will give you feedback, knowing you will not reprimand them for doing so. Create that environment of trust with people by telling them, "I really need your feedback because if I don't hear it, I won't improve." Turning your back and attacking, badmouthing, or throwing them under the bus because they gave you feedback is poor leadership at best and leadership malpractice at worst. It boils down to where you are on the crux, what you believe about people and their intentions, and your ability to not take the feedback personally but to accept and appreciate it as a necessary step toward your improvement.

The role of feedback in building a culture is explored further in chapter 10, "Culture."

HR TOOLS FOR PHYSICIANS AND CEOS

There are two ways to think about self-development: one is horizontal, and one is vertical. Horizontal self-development focuses on IQ-related elements—information, skills, and competencies. Conversely, vertical development focuses more on who we are—the sophisticated ways in which we think and show up, and everything needed to influence, inspire, and motivate others. Often, we focus on the horizontal because it's what we know and is relatively easy to continue developing. Vertical self-development requires a paradigm shift in how we learn about development.

Physicians must fundamentally change and lead in a different way, but they also must embrace this vertical development piece, which is much more difficult. It requires a lot of vulnerability and introspection. In that sense, we must move into EQ development versus relying solely on IQ.

EMOTIONAL INTELLIGENCE

In *Emotional Intelligence and Organizational Effectiveness,* Dr. Kalpana Srivastava provides this description:

Emotional intelligence can best be described as the ability to monitor one's own and other people's emotions, to discriminate between different emotions and label them appropriately, and to use emotional information to guide thinking and behavior.[2]

Another description of emotional intelligence comes from Mayer, Salovey, and Caruso, whose work was later popularized by Daniel Goleman:

Emotional Intelligence includes the ability to engage in sophisticated information processing about one's own and others' emotions and the ability to use this information as a guide to thinking and behavior. That is, individuals high in emotional intelligence pay attention to, use, understand, and manage emotions, and these skills serve adaptive functions that potentially benefit themselves and others.[3]

Put simply, EQ entails the ability to manage our own emotions, as well as sense the emotions and feelings of those

---

2   Kalpana Srivastava, "Emotional intelligence and organizational effectiveness," *Industrial Psychiatry Journal,* July–December 2013, accessed January 1, 2018, https://www.ncbi.nlm.nih.gov/pmc/articles/PMC4085815.

3   John D. Mayer, Peter Salovey and David R. Caruso, "Emotional Intelligence: New Ability or Eclectic Traits?" *American Psychologist,* 63, no. 6 (September 2008): 503–517.

around us, and then respond appropriately with kindness, understanding, and presence.

A study examined the correlation between low EQ in physicians and higher rates of errors and lawsuits. The study saw lower patient satisfaction and poorer outcomes with physicians who have lower EQs, as well as a positive correlation between physicians' EQs and their own job satisfaction. As the physician's EQ improves, so does their job satisfaction and overall professional motivation. According to the study,

> As the health system pivots from volume to value-based incentives that depend on team-based methods of care delivery and use of technologies in diagnosis, treatment and care coordination, a systemic approach to EQ in patient care needs thoughtful implementation.[4]

Thus, as we move closer and closer to team-based care, EQ is absolutely first and foremost on the minds of many leaders who want to shift that dynamic. Improving one's emotional intelligence necessitates a disciplined pursuit of self-awareness. Before you can make changes in yourself, you need a true understanding of who you are at your core, the feelings, emotions, and thoughts that drive

---

4   Paul Keckley and Marina Karp, "Emotional Intelligence Depends on More than Physician Behavior," *Hospitals and Health Networks*, May 17, 2016, accessed January 1, 2018, https://www.hhnmag.com/articles/7261-emotional-intelligence-depends-on-more-than-physician-behavior.

your behaviors. Only through this work can we begin to make improvements.

To aid in this discovery process, several assessments are available and can provide leaders with needed insights. The EQ-i, currently on its 2.0 version, is based on the Bar-On model of emotional intelligence and focuses on emotionally intelligent behaviors. The EQ-i is widely used in both research and business settings. This is not specifically for physicians; it's for anyone, and as of the writing of this book, I am not aware of any physician-specific EQ tests. It measures both emotional and social competencies of people's overall emotional intelligence and gives them very specific opportunities for development. More specifically, it looks at self-perception, self-expression, interpersonal skills, decision-making, and stress management. This tool also gives a well-being indicator, which is important, specifically as we deal with physician burnout and resiliency issues.

The EQ-i has a self-report option, so you can take the assessment yourself to get an introspective view. It also has a 360 option, so you can receive feedback from people around you, which, in my perspective, is necessary. If you don't get feedback from others, your self-report can leave some gaping holes in your realistic perspective of your emotional intelligence at work. MHS Assessments provides more details about this test on their website (https://ei.mhs.com/eqi2othescience.aspx).

Regarding EQ test utility in the development process, I've seen emotional intelligence assessments used very effectively as EQ relates to high-potential leaders. People hoping to move into a leadership role can gain initial awareness into their EQ blind spots as well as the strengths they can leverage. This works for everyone, all the way up to executive teams, where they may be used in conjunction with executive coaching. At this level, the 360 option gives some wonderfully specific insights that people don't hear during their day-to-day feedback and is rigorous enough to highlight detailed nuances of behaviors and characteristics.

The depth of the work here is often challenging and not for the faint of heart. Leaders who are hesitant to go into this level of self-discovery and conversation need a trusted partner to help them move through the process.

A skilled coach, whether internal or external to your organization, can be your greatest asset in this work. An honest and outside perspective provides you with a different point of view and will challenge you to question your beliefs and assumptions.

Too frequently in some organizations, when people start talking about coaching, the general attitude is, "What did you do wrong?" "What happened there?" But without coaching, leaders are not going to improve their skills. Don't be afraid of improving yourself. This body of knowledge and improvement should be intrinsic to anyone and everyone who seeks to be a successful leader.

In organizations that respect EQ to a high degree, the executive team adheres to the idea that they need to work on their emotional intelligence, they want to support it, and their colleagues from internal departments such as Learning and Development or HR can help facilitate the process. Additionally, external coaches can be a valuable resource to support this development and often can point out cultural nuances that may go unnoticed by internal partners.

As necessary as EQ is, the ability to assess, evaluate, and improve is a commitment. You can't simply host a conference and promise everyone they'll have higher EQs by the end of the day. A lot of self-learning and self-awareness, which of course is part of EQ, goes into this process. This type of development can take you from the gold level to the platinum level of leadership. This is not something you study, master, and then move on, like improving your knowledge of market dynamics. This is a long-term commitment of development. If you want to go from pretty good to excellent, you must be willing to evolve.

SOCIAL STYLES

Social Styles, one of the world's leading behavioral style models, is another useful assessment to gain self-awareness and insight into team dynamics. Imagine your team as people on a bus. Having a balanced mosaic of people with different social styles is key. The Social Styles Assessment is used all over the world and is based on over twenty years of research on successful teams and successful performances. It looks at preferences, individuals' preferred way of thinking and making decisions, and how people prefer to show up for work. After years of research into workplace success and individual behaviors, they find people fall into one of four unique styles: Analytical, Amiable, Driver, and Expressive.

In general, each style is linked to two different approaches. The first is whether a person asserts themselves more regularly in conversations or if that individual tends to wait and respond. One way to think of this is on a continuum of ask to tell. Reflect on your own tendencies. Do you normally ask questions or is your preference to tell others what is on your mind? The second is whether a person displays a lot of emotion or is more controlled. Again, you can reflect on your own style and see if your normal tendency is to emote, as in others can clearly see your reactions based on your emotions and physical expressions, or if you are controlled in your response, as in having much more of a poker-face approach that doesn't allow for others to read your emotions as clearly.

If an entire team took the assessment, they would obtain a better understanding of how each member thrives. Heather may show up as an Amiable. Jack may show up as an Expressive. One of its feature components allows people to see how they best interact with one another, as well. It stresses the importance of meeting people where they're at. If I know Jack is an Expressive, I can cater to that whether it's in meetings, hearing what his perspective is, or reflecting on it. If I were working with a Driver, I would need to come into meetings with a direct attitude. The strategy is completely different.

The versatility factor of social styles relates to the idea that you must be able to play in all four styles. A skillful leader is not only able to be kind of in the amiable space, the analytic space, the driver space, and the expressive space, but they're able to flex into those spaces without acting too much like a chameleon. They're skillful in how they approach these conversations. Presumably, versatility correlates highly with emotional intelligence.

You do not have to be pathetically aware of everything or try to make everybody happy. That's not the idea. It's about truly listening to what people say and understanding where they come from, regardless of how different your social styles are. Awareness and adaptability will infinitely aid you as a leader.

This training has great endurance as a group camaraderie learning exercise. If you give a group of people a tutorial on social styles, you will hear them reference it every day thereafter, giving them a common and shared language to solidify the learning. In corporate America, it's interesting to watch a group process their social styles both individually and in groups. Knowing yourself is very powerful.

There is not one more advantageous style; style is not good or bad. In certain cultures, certain styles do better. If people are simply aware of their style, it changes and perhaps improves the dynamic between individuals. It fosters an appreciation and understanding of conflicts and offers actionable strategies to help teams function more effectively.

The goal of surveys and assessments is to help you understand who you are, who you work with, and how you can work better. You don't need to employ every test, but find scientific surveys you understand and trust. In terms of what you can do to understand and better yourself, there is the emotional intelligence assessment, as we have discussed. You can also employ a Hogan Assessment, one of the few surveys based on research and capable of predicting performance. It has utility in the world of physician leadership. In the spaces of recruitment and development, assessors have been able to identify certain characteristics, traits, and attributes that predict higher performance for physician leaders. Therefore, people can recruit more intentionally toward the elements they wish to bring into their organization.

Self-awareness can be a major component of leading difficult changes, and difficult changes are part of doing business. Any organization that cares about its survival doesn't sit back without implementing change for years on end.

DEVELOPING YOUR TEAM

Developing yourself as a leader also involves hiring and developing teams, and future leaders within those teams. This is a new skillset for physician leaders, who are not used to being tasked with recruiting and training leaders, versus clinicians—the people who will surround them, support them, and complement their own strengths and weaknesses. As you evaluate your team, look for the key skills you're missing and need to be successful. Most physician leaders are used to elevated levels of personal competence and may be threatened when someone smart comes in alongside them, but it's necessary to do so as a physician leader.

When it comes to accepting and embracing those who have something to offer that I do not, regardless of their diverse backgrounds, attitudes, and personalities, I always keep in mind that I'm not a content expert in many areas. That's not humility; it's reality. Therefore, I don't surround myself with people who fawn over me, saying, "Oh Jack, that was brilliant. I can't believe you're so smart." I try to bring strength to the people who work alongside me, and then, hopefully, create a culture based on authenticity.

When I became president of the Colorado Permanente Medical Group in 1999, we had several challenges ahead of us. For the previous few years, we had experienced significant losses of membership, major financial losses, and had broad internal dissatisfaction marked by worsening physician (and other employee) satisfaction surveys and significant turnover in primary care. The breadth of these challenges combined with a newly forming team and my own inexperience meant I had to build in some very diverse skills and directions for the new executives I was assembling.

The team had three branches. Two vice presidents made up the first branch and oversaw reconstructing the culture and soul of the physician group to improve service to patients and members. This would be difficult, long-term work to improve morale and develop a positive can-do culture with improved patient experience. These two leaders worked tirelessly with all the physician leaders and clinicians with profound respect and passion. The second branch also included two people who were meant to find money in multiple ways that didn't undermine the mission or values of the organization. This included deep dives into revenues, expenses, all forms of contracting, and the very difficult conversations around variation in clinical practice. These two were superb and dedicated. An operations manager, a quality manager, and a finance manager comprised the third branch, which was responsible for keeping the ship afloat. I honor all seven of these highly capable individuals for their dedication to their individual responsibilities and their willingness to give the others the space and time to pursue goals that often were quite different in both focus and time frame.

We had three branches and seven people with extremely different knowledge, and I knew there wasn't a single path for us to take directed from just one smart person. Neither I nor any of them was that one smart person. My decision to put together a team with such extremely different perspectives was based on the fact that we could not save money with such a low morale, and we could not improve morale without saving money.

Because I didn't have the answers, I added extremes to the team and said, "Here's the reality. We're all in this together, and we have to figure it out." We weren't singing "Kumbaya" in six months; we still had conflict, and it was certainly an interesting ride. But because I didn't let them caucus me separately and we met together regularly, they had to listen to each other. We had off-sites at my cabin, and we did all kinds of activities where they had to be together. I think in the end, they would have all said they learned a lot from each other.

These off-site meetings were vital because we spent time diving deep into key questions, like, "What does this mean for our team? How do we improve our performance? Then how will that increase results?" That's an overlooked piece in a lot of organizations. They provide surveys but don't give people the time to integrate what they've learned.

You can develop a team in a variety of ways; there are many pathways to success. I don't believe in the chummy attitude of always doing everything together, but I do believe in finding meaningful ways to organize, socialize, go off-site, and learn from one another. When building my team, we went to my mountain cabin to meet and discuss many different strategic initiatives but also engaged in an extra activity that proved to be exceptionally useful from a team development perspective: cooking together.

One of the money-finders was an epicurean cook, concert

pianist, master woodworker, and a scratch golfer. The perfection gene went so deep in his DNA that he was appalled by my pots and pans. Others were not very comfortable in the kitchen, but all learned as we went along, and the experience revealed contrasting personal styles and biases. So they were antithetical in terms of their approach. The chef was always concerned with getting everything done in a timely matter. He had a drive-to-the-top-of-the-hill mentality. Others, however, believed in helping everyone get to the top of the hill without stepping on their feet as you walked. These observations and lessons were learned in a very humorous environment. We learned that some people were very good at setting tables and doing dishes. That would be me.

Cooking dinner and breakfast was always fun. We all disagreed and wanted different things, but we had to succeed somehow, so we had to work together. This seemingly benign activity of cooking and breaking bread together highlighted each of our unique gifts through a new and insightful lens, and allowed our team to find new opportunities to work together and support one another that didn't happen in the workplace.

WHY LEVEL 5 LEADERSHIP IS A KEY COMPONENT FOR DEVELOPING GREAT LEADERS AND TEAMS

Based on the findings of Jim Collins and others, Level 5

leadership is an ideal state for the best leaders. Collins describes Level 5 leaders as fiercely focused on the problems but also humble and understanding of people and their issues.

In his 2001 *Harvard Business Review* article and his book *Good to Great*, Collins notes that Level 5 leaders have all the abilities of the other four levels, plus a unique blend of extreme personal humility with intense personal will. This is what sets apart the Level 5 leader.

In *Good to Great*, Collins also discusses the Stockdale Paradox. Admiral Stockdale was the longest-held prisoner of war in the Vietnam War. He was tortured more than twenty times during his eight-year imprisonment, from 1965 to 1973. Per Collins, he also "shouldered the burden of command, doing everything he could to create conditions that would increase the number of prisoners who would survive unbroken, while fighting an internal war against his captors."[5] He had seen people die and he had seen people survive. When he came out, he was keen on understanding why.[6]

The Stockdale Paradox encompassed a profound understanding of reality described as such: You know exactly

---

5   Jim Collins, *Good to Great: Why Some Companies Make the Leap and Others Don't* (New York: HarperCollins, 2001), 83.

6   Collins, *Good to Great.*

what's going on. You're not thinking something will magically happen to change your situation. The second half of the equation is a quiet resolve that you will endure. You have the resolve and resilience to endure what's happening and take it one day at a time. This is relevant because some of the people who died did neither. They gave up, or as Stockdale put it, "They died of a broken heart. Their mentality was: 'This is bad, but I know our guys are going to figure this out and we'll be out by Christmas." Christmas came and went, and they spiraled into a cycle of hope and despair, hope and despair. Eventually, they died.

Stockdale said, "You must never confuse faith that you will prevail in the end—which you can never afford to lose—with the discipline to confront the most brutal facts of your current reality, whatever they might be."[7]

I often think of the Stockdale Paradox when leading change. For example, if Medicare cuts our income by 20 percent, we face an absolute reality that we cannot change. The law has passed. That's it. If that's it, what are we going to do? Are we going to say, "We've been harmed. It's awful. It's terrible. We're going to wait until the world gets better or we're going to wait until they wake up in Washington"? Or are we going to say, "This is reality. We better hang in there. This is on our watch. This is our responsibility. How do we work together?" The

7   Collins, *Good to Great*, 84.

Stockdale Paradox notion of a brutal understanding of reality is very much what the Level 5 leader understands, which is, "I'm not going to make this an emotional issue, but this is exactly what's going on, and I can't change it by wishing it was different." Then, Level 5 leaders tap into their unrelenting faith that in the end they will prevail and act to make things better.

It's also worth noting that Level 5 leadership is not extreme; it's honest humility, and not for the sake of self-deprecation. It's authentic humility coupled with an amazing desire and professional will to not accept mediocrity and to push yourself to continue building superb, industry-leading results. The yin and yang of humility and that unrelenting desire for improvements and success is a paradoxical combination of traits of highly successful leaders.

That honesty is integral to the combination because, in my experience, humility has become cool. You often see audacious or arrogant people who claim to be humble, as if it's trendy to display humility, but the genuine trait requires real depth. Often, when folks put on a show, you can feel the insincerity, which is merely self-serving. Your first clue is when they use the word "humility" or "humble." Self-promoting people might proclaim they're humbled when something good happens to them, and while I believe they're appreciative, that's not the same as humility.

CHAPTER 6

LEADERSHIP TRAITS AND EXPECTATIONS AND TEAMBUILDING

Physician leaders are more likely to succeed if they have certain traits, most of which are attributable to themselves as a person but are also linked to their profession.

LEADERSHIP TRAITS

1. Highly respected clinician
2. Integrity
3. Emotional intelligence
4. Humility

That first trait is being highly respected as a clinician. This is the initial platform on which they will be viewed and judged. This includes their basic clinical skills, but also how they carry themselves professionally as a colleague, caregiver, and trusted member of the professional community. If one is not respected for their basic professional craft, it is a weak platform from which to lead, especially with issues that are controversial or challenging to one's professional colleagues. Once a physician accepts the responsibility of leadership, that new skillset must be developed for colleagues to have confidence in them in the new role.

The number two desirable trait for physician leaders is integrity, which is important because trust is the currency of both leadership and communication, and trust is earned over time. It comes from a person's basic integrity, but it can be lost very quickly. Integrity is the spine of your leadership, and unwavering adherence to values over time leads to trust.

Number three is emotional intelligence. We don't always look to the smartest person in the room because it's not enough to be bright, or even to be right. Intellectual superiority is a nice platform, but it can also denigrate people around you. Trying to depend on outsmarting people is a very difficult pathway. As we discussed in chapter 5, a leader's ability to be self-aware, empathetic, and respectful helps to create the positive culture that's so important in health care. We are selected for our profession based heavily on academic prowess, so leadership training is critical and emotional intelligence—including managing yourself—is how we become trusted and effective.

🔑 KEY POINT

It's not enough to be bright.

It's not even enough to be right.

You need to be effective.

The fourth trait is humility. This trait is not always present, but it is a great enabler and gives the leader a style that is readily useful, especially when leaders have some of their most trying and difficult problems and proposed solutions. It's a powerful trait when it is quietly authentic. Humility is not about being meek or weak, and it is not passive. It is a genuine sense of yourself, with both integrity and respect for others.

TWIN REFLECTION: HUMILITY PERSONIFIED

I was in a sixteen-hour surgery, separating two little conjoined twins. If we were an orchestra, I would have been the fourth violin. I was a CEO, but I was in there as an assistant to the assistant to the assistant plastic surgeon, helping when I could as activity bustled around us. People were doing important work, and I was struck by how two specific doctors performed so radically differently from one another. One surgeon was noisy and loud, reminding me of a peacock. Everything centered on him. That was made more obvious because the entire day was filmed for local TV.

The other surgeon was very quiet and focused on the work. He checked in on other people on the surgical team and had this tremendous strength. He genuinely respected the responsibilities and roles of his colleagues and had an almost professional reverence for the patients and the family. We all were influenced by the unique challenge of this rare operation and the continuous attention in the room, but this surgeon was clearly focused on everything but him.

I went home that night and wrote a poem, "Twin Reflection."

Arrogance is the wayward twin of confidence. Arrogance is self-promoting and needy. Confidence is humble and secure. Arrogance is noisy, yet weak. Confidence is quiet, yet strong. Arrogance tries to be interesting. Confidence seeks to be interested.

We talk about confidence and arrogance as almost interchangeable. If you saw both traits together at play, you would be able to discern the differences. I wrote this as a tribute to my colleague who was the confident one. I had a calligrapher write it up, frame it, and then, on Christmas Eve, I called my colleague and asked to drop something off.

His wife greeted me, we all had a glass of cheer, and I said, "I want to show you what I brought you for Christmas."

His wife exclaimed, "What did you bring for Berry?"

I told her I wrote a poem inspired by her husband.

She laughed and said, "Well, you two are quite a pair!"

What Berry modeled in the operating room that night was the true power of humility.

I also look for passion in physician leaders. The first side of passion is enthusiastic belief. In other words, you're there because you want to be, and you believe in what you do. The other side of passion is resolve. After you've been kicked around a couple of times, you must be able to access that enthusiastic belief. Where is that enthusiastic belief? This is resolve. It can carry a leader through the most trying problems, and it is most effective when it is rooted in our belief system and our sense of personal mission.

Highly respected physicians are important, integrity and emotional intelligence are important, and humility and passion are important, but something needs to tie these elements together in a way that serves the patients. A physician leader's true north should be valuing the patient, remembering that the role of the patient is involuntary—no one wakes up trying to become one. Physicians and physician leaders are their trusted partners in this journey. Patients deserve improvement in their lives and in their experience with our system. That is your purpose. You are there for the patient. This focus bridges this section on leadership traits and the next section on leadership expectations, so both serve the true north of the responsibilities of healer, leader, and partner.

KEY LEADERSHIP EXPECTATIONS

Having most or all the desired traits is important, to optimize that a leader can succeed in the challenges they will face. But to provide clarity of what success will look like and require, it is important that the expectations associated with the role are well-defined. These are the leadership expectations which will be important, and they will have associated specific goals and measures.

PERFORMANCE

Wherever you work, you are part of a system. The leadership team and the board need to agree on what matters to the system. What is important? What do we live and die for? What do we stand for? These begin to define how we will measure the performance of the organization. Then we must decide on the right values and expectations for those who work there and determine what the standards are and how to measure them. Promising ideas and intentions are fine, but you can only improve what you measure.

The process of agreeing on what matters often starts with identifying your values. Leaders must ask, "What is our mission, and where do we need to go?" Then, they can evaluate what they must do to get there. Doctors need to be dedicated to patients, efficient, and safe so they can come up with reasonable expectations. That's a process the leadership must carry out. It should be inclusive of the target, the subjects, and the physicians. They should at least have some direct contact with these groups or a survey where they are heard. Decide what you are going to measure, and then apply those, measure them, and monitor them. While organizations will determine their prioritized measures, they may typically include areas of clinical quality, service, access, professionalism, and commitments to affordability and efficiency, and the standard business parameters, including finances and growth. The first time you do this, you should clearly communicate it's a learning cycle. You have put measurements in place, will monitor what you learn, and find ways to improve. It's an integrative process and a circle of continuous learning and improvement.

Formalizing and transparently measuring expectations provide the basis for measuring performance and monitoring progress. In chapter 8, "Performance Management," we discuss this in detail, including an important emphasis of understanding the four groups who always suffer when performance issues are not taken seriously.

COMMUNICATION

The second expectation of leaders is communication, which is intrinsically linked to credibility. In many ways, as stated previously, leadership *is* communication. Leaders are here to create a continuous conversation of learning, acknowledgment, and challenge to reinforce the process of team and individual continuous learning together, and cocreating information and solutions.

As we mentioned earlier, credibility is based on our ability to influence others. However, the ability to influence others makes you only partially credible. True credibility also demands that you demonstrate your willingness and ability to be influenced—to listen. Too many people believe they have enough genius and confidence to forgo listening, which is incredibly insufficient. This is where genuine humility becomes important. If you don't understand that others have an enormous contribution to make—an enormous knowledge base, insight base, and experience base—then you miss many details, new facts, nuances, and frank corrections.

Communicating effectively often requires repeating and reinforcing messages. Communication is much more longitudinal than episodic—it's a commitment over time rather than an action in the moment.

Customized messaging versus situational truth: A delicate challenge for leaders is the ability to customize content for different audiences to ensure that the proper messages are delivered within the group's reality without actually morphing the core messages toward a more situational truth designed to pacify or manipulate. This would undermine the credibility of the leader and reflect negatively on their integrity. Anticipate this reality and the best way to customize the content without manipulation.

LEARNING

Learning is a fundamental leadership expectation. To respond to the magnitude and difficulties of change, we need this continuous process of open learning for ourselves and our teams. Leaders must create models for this, both for yourself and for those who follow you, and actively participate, demonstrating that you not only require learning but are very committed. This can be accomplished through book clubs, lectures, off-sites, blogs, and group learning, and by convening diverse types of groups—not just classic leadership structures but signal generators.

SIGNAL GENERATORS

Over time in an organization, a formal leadership structure develops based on departmental, facility, regional, or other structural features, and there is both formality of structure and function, and some levels of hierarchy and reporting. But as senior leaders commit to understanding problems and people more clearly, we are also aware of a more informal leadership structure based on credibility and influence and trust. These are the trusted colleagues whose opinions and feedback are always sought by the everyday work teams. This informal group is incredibly important, so creating a process to hear from them and have them spend time with formal leaders is valuable. Two of my vice presidents, Drs. Patty Fahy and Andy Lum, proposed this model and led the development.

A model that worked for us, to provide a platform for these people, was to assemble the formal leaders and then post a large list of informal leaders who were well understood to be the most trusted voices and sought-after opinions in the group. There is always overlap when you talk about trust and credibility with formal leaders. But once the lengthy list of informal leaders is created, a simple prioritizing exercise can be carried out. This can be as simple as giving each of the formal leaders five sticky dots and having them apply those dots to the names of the informal leaders whom they believe has the greatest trust and credibility. This exercise can then yield a new subset that all agree they want to hear more from. You now have a group of formal leaders and a group of informal signal generators.

The next step is to organize each group informally to have some spokespeople and partners to select topics, define venues, and convene the group for a gathering. The notion of egalitarian self-governance for this group can yield great energy, and a series of gatherings to define topics and share views can be a great unearthing of the most critical issues. How often a group like this meets and how long they stay together is 100 percent governed by the group. It's up to the group to find and identify the value in it.

We model learning by what we do and try to do. If we don't model it, then we'll never have people believe in it. You must set the example.

The signal generators exercise was powerful. Eventually, people decided they didn't need to continue as a large, formal group. Not every individual in the formal group had to be involved in every discussion, so the signal generators dispersed.

I believe the greatest value gained by developing the group was the individual relationships it created. Some players chose to continue those relationships, meeting in smaller groups as needed.

RESOLVE

As a leader, you must have resolve. As previously described, resolve is the other side of passion, in which you remain strong in the face of difficulties. Additionally, this relates to Level 5 leadership, in which you must have grit and face reality head-on.

Sidney Garfield had resolve. So did Admiral Stockdale, who was the longest-held prisoner of war in the Vietnam War, and Dr. Viktor E. Frankl, who escaped from a concentration camp, and like Stockdale, wrote about why some people survived the most deplorable environments while others did not. Frankl said, "The one thing you can't take away from me is the way I choose to respond to what you do to me."[1]

Like Admiral Stockdale, Dr. Sidney Garfield, or Dr. Viktor Frankl, to be a leader, you must embrace reality with clarity and the personal resolve to proceed.

LEADERSHIP MYTHS

A massive myth about physician leaders is that they must be business content experts—that for the physician leader to be competent and relevant, they must possess equivalent knowledge around finance, strategy, and marketing. This isn't true, but be sure you have team members you

---

1   Viktor E. Frankl, *Man's Search for Meaning* (Boston: Beacon Press, 2006).

trust who *are* competent in this area and can convene with you. Subject-matter experts are important, but you don't have to internalize everything yourself. Know where they are, trust them, and work with them. In fact, the inherent diversity of expertise between various disciplines, including clinical, is powerful.

CLINICAL DECISION PROCESS AND TRAINING WORKS IN BUSINESS

We spend so much energy trying to get clinicians to understand the business process and model when, in fact, the clinical model works very nicely in the business world. The clinical model of decision-making is useful in business decisions and strategy. The delivery of care and approach to a patient and a diagnosis is similar: you gather the data, you do the necessary exams and tests, and you arrive at a diagnosis so you may examine potential solutions. That's not different from business, where you have a diagnosis and you look at potential solutions.

In clinical medicine, we look for the indications, alternatives, risks, and possible complications. If we say we're treating you for a brain tumor, we'd better know what the indications are, the alternatives—radiation, surgery, chemo—the risks, and the possible complications. That's the clinical model. We can apply this model in business. We examine the indications, alternatives, risks, and possible complications of a business decision such as a strategy.

As a leader in the business, the clinical point of view is a gift. It's about decision-making.

The mythology is you must be an expert on everything, which is simply untrue. You need enough information to ask good questions, have a clinical point of view that can be helpful to continue building a relationship where we learn together, and the competence that comes from shared knowledge.

Another myth about leadership is that you always have to be right—or that it's not acceptable to be wrong. Let me use a story to elucidate this.

I was invited to a transition off-site of a large medical group in California. Their current president was leaving, their new president was coming in, and they invited four of us to speak to the group. The four people who spoke were the outgoing president, a president from another region, me as the national leader, and a business consultant. We all gave talks, and then the moderator asked each of us to offer our best advice to the incoming president.

The outgoing president was very stern and said, "You have to show the insurance leaders that you won't get pushed over. Stand up to them so they know you're engaged and they can't make decisions without you." While that was basically true, and we do need to be tough when it is required, we also must learn the power of collaboration.

The consultant was next, and she had a very severe style, with a frown on her face and a seriousness that permeated everything. She said, "Well, Doctor, you're moving into the business world, which is different from your world. You have to know marketing like the marketing people and finance like the finance people. Otherwise, they will not take you seriously." I was shocked—and grateful she had not checked off on my own candidacy and credentials when the Colorado region selected me as their president.

Finally, I thought I had some latitude and knew what to say when the other regional president stood. He said, "You have to realize you don't know it all. You're going to have to develop a talented team, learn with them, and learn from them."

I thought to myself, "You rascal, that was exactly the answer I was going to provide!" To buy myself a little time, I said, "Thanks, Doctor. That was actually *my* answer. So, well done."

I could have simply said the two of us agreed and moved on, but I continued. "Actually, Jeff, I have another thought. I know you're a courageous, smart guy. You have determination and bias for action and results that can make me feel frail by comparison. You are driven, and I admire that. I believe that you are going to be courageous and bold in making tremendous changes. But what happens when you make substantial changes and you're new? Or even if you're not brand-new, but you make substantial changes? As smart as you are and as good as the advice is you receive, over time, some of those decisions are not going to work out. Your hypothesis may be wrong, or your solution may be flawed, or your execution may be imperfect, but you make big, bold decisions to go forward and do something and it doesn't work out. And that is going to be the moment of great reflection for you. We are tempted to deny, minimize, or blame, rather than openly acknowledge what transpired. The combination of substantial risk, bold solution, advanced clearly by you and an unquestioned failure to solve the problems creates a large personal shock and you are at risk of saying to yourself, 'It wasn't worth it. Next time I will only take half as much risk.'"

But we need Jeff to continue being bold and taking risks.

I continued, "I think this is the path you should consider: 'I was wrong. I am going to take this time with my team and understand the issues we were wrong about. Was it our thinking, our design, our data gathering, our solution set, or our execution that was wrong? What do we need to learn?' Do that and then take the next step to get your risk tolerance from 50 percent back to 100 percent."

You will find yourself in this situation, and when you do, forgive yourself—knowing you did everything you could—then learn from the experience and move on. That forgiveness is crucial.

Do not minimize the pain associated with failure. That pain is real, and you have to absorb the hard, painful lesson before you can move on. At some point, though, take a deep breath and forgive yourself. You are human.

This expression of forgiveness is not about falling down and saying, "I am not worthy." Rather, it is a thoughtful acknowledgment of the brutal facts and the learning and a rededication to, and belief in, yourself.

I have seen others have grand ideas that fell flat, and they spent their energy blaming others, while the real internal message was, "Never again." That moment of personal forgiveness, after a thorough learning debrief, is crucial.

Consider a situation where a surgeon operates on a patient and makes a terrible mistake, the patient dies, and the doctor, racked with guilt, is unable to forgive themselves. There is a stark reality to how we manage disappointment and failure in this. Personal forgiveness is very important, but there's a price. You must acknowledge it's your fault, not someone else's, or you'll never allow yourself to go back to 100 percent in terms of your willingness to take risks. If you become too accustomed to failing and blaming others, that's even more terrifying because then it becomes part of your skillset.

From Sheryl Sandberg, writing about Facebook:

> To be resilient after failures, we have to learn from them. Most of the time we know this; we just don't do it. We're too insecure to admit mistakes to ourselves or too proud to admit them to others. Instead of opening up, we get defensive and shut down. A resilient organization helps people overcome these reactions by creating a culture that encourages individuals to acknowledge their missteps and regrets... The majority of regrets were about failures to act, not actions that failed. Psychologists have found that over time we usually regret the chances we missed, not the chances we took.[2]

The Marines make formal debriefs a routine part of their evaluation of every training exercise, sitting together to discuss failure in excruciating detail and recording, publicly, all the learning. They have created a culture where failure is a learning opportunity when feedback is expected, required, and focused on the facts—hard lessons. This kind of process has been developed in health care in our mortality and morbidity conferences

---

2   Sheryl Sandberg and Adam Grant, *Option B: Facing Adversity, Building Resilience, and Finding Joy* (New York: Knopf, 2017), 144-145.

but should be broadly embraced as a key component of a culture of learning.

Again, you don't always have to be right. And when you're not right, it's not a failure; it's a hypothesis, plan, and execution that has some serious faults. It is a myth that you must always be right. You must adopt a culture of learning, take risks, and forgive together. That's not a culture of weakness.

THE FIVE C'S OF LEADERSHIP

These characteristics are grouped here for the leader to ponder and reflect upon as the day-to-day journey of challenges and realities evolves and grows.

CLARITY

Clarity is the number one behavior of leadership because it provides people with a solid base upon which to agree or disagree. If people are not sure what you think, they give you responses you may not be able to use. Clarity is not often a strong trait for leaders because it involves being clear with yourself and taking a stand. It gives people solid ground to follow you or a factual basis to disagree with you, and to provide you with their important experience and opinion. Leaders can drive people crazy if they lack clarity. I see leaders dancing around a subject, waffling on their opinions, and changing their message back and forth, which creates tremendous uncertainty among their audience. Ambiguity can suck the energy out of a group, so clarity is important.

 **KEY POINT**

Don't get mad at someone for not doing what you never clearly asked them to do.

—DR. PATTY FAHY

You need to emphasize clarity from the very beginning, after you share context, to come to a shared understanding of what the problem and the solution are. If you are unclear and start with a solution, you miss input from people who would enthusiastically agree or disagree with you.

If you have not done the necessary work to be certain of your own point of view, it will be very apparent and confusing to your audience. Again, it's not about being correct or superior in your knowledge but getting to a workable solution. Start with your own premise, which may be, 'I have no idea. Help me.' That is true clarity.

KEY POINT

In order to be convincing, you first must be convinced.

CONSISTENCY

The people and organization you lead and serve will value and appreciate consistency. This is not about just being boringly mundane or not believing in creativity and innovation. It is about truly knowing who someone is based on their repeated behaviors—having trust that someone will show up and be the same person they were a week ago. You trust these people because they are consistent. You have a reliable relationship. They have consistency of character and values. Creativity and innovation can complement this trait quite well.

COLLABORATION

I am on the board of University of California San Francisco Institute for Global Health Sciences. They have determined that one of the greatest deficiencies in global health is a lack of collaboration. They ask, "Well, what does that mean?"

Drive down a dusty road in the middle of East Africa, and you might see a church sponsored by an organization. Behind the church is a backhoe for digging, which they use to build more churches. Two miles down the road, you'll see a school sponsored by another organization. They dig by hand because they don't use the church's unused backhoe, but they have a truck that they rarely use, which would be of use to the church if offered.

Those kinds of occurrences happen all the time where resources are limited, but people don't openly recognize and share them.

Collaboration is often missing in health care. We have a history and culture that encourages physicians to function individually rather than as a team. We compete, stemming from a background of individual education, training, corporate structure, and measurement. Frankly, it is bad modeling. This is where you miss the opportunity to say, "If I actually had a little bit more of a network, a coalition of learning colleagues, I could do some of this myself, as well as recruit others to help."

This is not done well in medicine. We may be competitors on a certain level, but we must find ways to collaborate. If we continue in the overly competitive culture, we invariably run the risk of duplicating costs and taking unfocused, inefficient action.

Professor Morten Hansen wrote a book titled *Collaboration*. It is not simply about getting along; it's about finding ways to work with one another in a disciplined manner. For instance, two hospitals on the same block might want to build a cardiac center and an oncology center. Collaboration means deciding you will build one center while the other hospital builds the other center, as this is more efficient. You find ways to save money and improve by being disciplined in your collaborations. Duplication and oversupply are often major cost drivers in health care.

COMPASSION

As difficult as it gets, we all committed to this profession because we believed we were healers. If we don't continuously display compassion for the issues and the people, shame on us. It is a chance to differentiate yourself as an individual.

If you are compassionate as a clinician, if you are a healer, you should also be compassionate as a team member and a boss because we are all stressed. Even though doctors may not be dying of a cancer, we are all experiencing something challenging called life. Compassion is a very nice trait in physician leadership because we come from a compassionate profession and should not lose that as we lead people.

Again, is it soft? Yes, probably. Is it strong? Very much so. As Merwyn Hayes, PhD, says, "Be tough on the issues and easy on the people."

COURAGE

Courage is a kindred characteristic to resolve. You have to show up. You must keep your values and responsibilities in clear view, and you must continue. Dust yourself off and keep going. We still have not solved enough problems for patients, and we must continue working.

A Kentucky Derby trainer once said, "Good horses win races when all the important factors work. Great horses win races when none of the important factors work."

While courage is often associated with an individual, leaders do not have an unlimited supply of it. We must remember the power of our teams and the support system they can provide to us. Our teams can recharge us by listening, understanding, providing counsel, and being there for us when we need a lot of courage. Leaders do not have to go it alone.

CHAPTER 7

THE DIFFICULT CROWD

❓ WICKED QUESTION

What are the silent ones observing, thinking, and concluding?

Are they listening silently and/or why aren't they engaging?

Leadership involves continuous communication and connectivity with constituents to both share important updates, changes, or contextual realities, and this means regular interaction with audiences to deliver messages and to hear feedback. These groups can vary from affably engaged to angry and challenging. Difficult groups are tests of a leader's ability to convey important messages, but more importantly to stay "with the group" when the topics, tone, and emotions get difficult and challenging so that the key learning can evolve without getting lost in emotional overreaction. Preparation and practice are keys for leaders to manage themselves to optimize results from meetings with the difficult crowd.

First, be prepared that while there may be three people attacking you and your message, remember there are another thirty-seven people in the room listening quietly. They are attentive and trying to understand who is really leading this situation and whom they want to believe in and follow.

⚡ VOLTAGE DROP

Leading is 24/7. After a challenging session working through complicated issues with the difficult crowd, the leader will inevitably feel a combination of relief, optimism, and even disappointment or anger. Ideally, the leader has managed themselves with great emotional intelligence, respect, and thoughtful exchanges. But there is a tendency after these events to unwind a bit by sharing some reactions with highly trusted colleagues, and that might occur in an elevator, hallway, or cafe. If the leader, while feeling they are engaging a trusted listener who will be fair and understanding, a high alert should be deployed to be aware that within earshot can be a number of people with a wide variety of knowledge and views. Getting on a crowded elevator and turning to a colleague and expressing negative comments about individuals or the group can travel throughout the elevator...and then everywhere!

Leaders develop strong, long-term allegiances with people in difficult crowds by how they manage the difficulties. They manage themselves, are authentic, and they listen. It's hard, but the third time is easier than the first time, and the tenth time is easier than the third. It's a matter of being aware, disciplined, and prepared.

First and foremost, you must show up. If you do not show up, you leave a void that nefarious activities or people fill. Even those who are unhappy with you will recognize that you didn't send someone else to listen to their complaints.

Then, you have to manage yourself. This ties in to how you relate to people, as well as being prepared for what will happen, and not being surprised when you encounter difficulties. Significant communication is not easily delegated. It sends the message that this will be too difficult for you to handle or not important enough for you to show up yourself. Part of showing up is symbolic. It means your topic of discussion matters. Having the wrong person show up is fraught with difficulties and is rarely done well. In dysfunctional senior teams, people receive different messages from the person who shows up in comparison to their boss or CEO. If you walk into the fire, you need to do it in your own shoes.

Communication is key here. It dictates how you manage yourself—how exactly you show up. It also fits in with the concept of continuous iterative sharing of context. You shouldn't simply expect to win a crowd over 100 percent. If you do, you face a separate set of problems.

As we have alluded to previously, because of our training, which requires precision and accuracy of science, physicians tend to be very discerning and even skeptical of new information, necessitating validation. When someone brings expertise to the table, there's generally some natural skepticism around trying to find the evidence behind their claims. It doesn't necessarily mean the individual who challenges the expert and expresses skepticism believes the expert is a bad person, but if they take the challenge personally, it creates a bad dynamic.

There is an authentic background for some of the negativity and skepticism. We are always challenging the truth because our science depends on it. It's not unusual or shocking that we receive pushback from colleagues. A certain baseline level of that is normal, but a disturbing amount isn't.

VALUE DISSENT AND CHALLENGE CRITICISM

When you face a room full of people, many of whom seem unhappy, you need to be calm enough to recognize that their views and behaviors are not uniform.

One group, which I refer to as the dissenters, will disagree with you. However, in the context of their disagreement, they offer other points of view and solutions. They are energized, forward-thinking, and usually respected among their peers. They will argue with you, tell you why you're wrong, and provide solutions that differ from yours. I have learned to highly value the dissenters, even though they can be very challenging and aggressive. While they can disagree and be unhappy with the logic or direction of leadership's decisions, their concern is focused on better thinking and outcomes to solve the problem rather than just complaining about the issues and leadership. The wise leader will learn that the contribution of the dissenter is golden.

Another group that will disagree with you is the cynics. Cynicism is quite different. This group may sit with their arms folded. They live in a reality of futility. Life sucks. It has always sucked. It still sucks, and by the way, you suck. They have neither energy nor solutions. They're simply unhappy. Wasting your time trying to cheer them up or convince them to see your point of view is a fool's errand, especially when there are other people in the room deserving of your attention—early adopters who want to discuss the improvements or dissenters who want to find a different solution. Those people want to be part of the conversations. The cynics don't, and so I will often say something I learned in a training course called Play to Win presented by the organization WolfCreek Partners: "In order to respond to you, can you turn that into a request? Ask me to do something, make it tangible, and be part of the forward thinking." Other times, I might acknowledge the cynic, let them know that I understand the topic is important to them and that they have a strong opinion, but that in the interest of time, we need to move on. I then offer them one-on-one time to discuss the matter further. When you do that, if they truly want to have a discussion, they will take you up on your offer.

Value the dissenters, but challenge the cynics.

When you're addressing an audience, a small group of disagreeable people—who I refer to as the agitators—might hook you with aggressive questions. Unlike the dissenters, they do not offer alternative solutions and you waste everyone's time by fighting them. You are obligated to understand the agitators but should not react too early or too forcefully. You must manage the time and experience of the entire group, and not disrespect those in the group with good intentions, by engaging in a mud-wrestling match with those seeking to hijack the conversation. It's easy to focus on those distractions, but the people who agree with you will likely sit quietly. They don't want to take these guys on either.

I have often walked out of rooms, only to be stopped by someone who says, "Thanks, Jack, I really agree with you."

"You got lockjaw?" I ask. "You were in there for an hour and you didn't say a word."

The common response is, "I wasn't going to stir those guys up."

Audience members can be quiet for a multitude of reasons. Maybe they simply don't have the energy to be upset that night. Perhaps they don't have enough information to form a solid opinion, or they don't want to get on the agitators' bad sides.

Finally, not everyone is an early adopter, a dissenter, a cynic, or an agitator all the time, and their attitudes can change over time. A person who is typically an early adopter may have just received some unwelcome news or is just having a difficult day. However, as the leader, it's your responsibility to manage the room and be respectful of everyone's time, while still trying to solve a problem.

I learned this through trial and error, by trying to manage myself out of my own discomfort and frustration. I'd wonder why people were so angry with me and why this was so difficult. I've made mistakes, but my default position has always been listening, which has helped me learn.

I learned how to not get locked down with the negative energy in the room, to listen for constructive yet opposing views, and to distinguish between the dissenters and the cynics. As a leader, it is your responsibility to not get locked into your own opinion or into the negativity of others, but to listen because your responsibility is not to your own opinion, you are responsible for the greater good of the organization.

🔑 KEY POINT

Value dissent, challenge cynicism.

You must manage time wisely in these scenarios, so sometimes you need to recognize their unhappiness and move on. Again, there are multiple kinds of groups in each crowd.

If the situation escalates, it's your job to remind people that, at the very least, you do expect good manners to guide the discussion. Remind people that you want to do the right thing and do what's right for the group, and while you may not all agree, a level of professional decorum is necessary to proceed in a constructive manner.

Addressing the difficult crowd also involves managing yourself. You're still in control of your emotions, and being incredibly transparent and honest, and so you have a right to expect the same from everyone else. When a session seems to be getting more dysfunctional, let them know that.

For example, you might say, "I want to talk about how this group wants to relate to itself. How are we going to treat each other around here? I know you disagree with me. I'm not trying to be disagreeable. Give me your ideas. Let's work on this together. I don't think we're going in different directions, and if you think we are, we can put that as a key topic. I'd like to take our energy level and focus on the problem and not just bicker with each other."

After these discussions, no matter where you are, you must always keep your role as a leader in mind. Never publicly complain about the difficult crowd.

Note the connection between self-awareness, knowing your own beliefs, and this discussion about behaviors to avoid around the difficult crowd. When dealing with tough crowds, don't attack, don't crumble, and don't commiserate. Those behaviors are unavailable to a leader who is not self-aware. If you don't understand what triggers you—what hooks you—you will never get ahead of your own reaction to attack. Much of managing the difficult crowd rests on your ability to understand yourself, your beliefs, and your triggers, and being able to catch those triggers before the triggers catch you.

MY PERSONAL MANTRA

My personal mantra while standing in front of a difficult, challenging group is, "Listen, acknowledge, and challenge." Never stop listening, acknowledge their words, and then add your information in your response to challenge them.

WHAT YOU NEED TO KNOW ABOUT THE EASY CROWD

The easy crowd is blessed and may be rare. They're engaged. They're aligned with the work being carried out by them or around them. They trust the leader and have constructive ideas in what they express. They're confident the leader will attend to their concerns.

The easy crowd is focused on improvement and being part of a better future and creating better solutions, and their dissent is animated but respectful and purposeful. There's just one caveat: don't accept their cheerfulness as an end state because occasionally this group's appearance of being happy and satisfied might be because they are underinformed and unaware of some of the crucial issues.

Maybe they're cheerful because they haven't heard the real news. You need to probe, test, and question this group to ensure their depth of understanding.

Your first reaction will be relief over an oasis of people who are cheerful, happy, and want to talk about a better future. Nobody is sneering or waiting for their chance to talk, and you're caught a little off guard. Don't thank them too soon, though, and then leave. Again, share context. Describe what you know and what you've learned. Add a little nuance. You're not just there to inform them. You're also on the cliff, telling them what's down in the valley. That's part of senior leadership: the role of riding a scout horse and warning them that while circumstances might appear bleak, once you pass the summit, this is how you'll see change. Don't leave the cheerful how you met them—ensure you're also communicating a message. You may need to probe to see what they do understand to be sure you can give them information to fill any critical gaps. Give them something to think about.

THREE TYPES OF DIFFICULT CROWDS

There are three types of difficult crowds. These divisions are a little artificial, but it helps to identify each one as you experience them. Again, when you go into a group of unhappy or unpleasant physicians, the third time is easier than the first time, and the tenth time is easier than the third time. Part of this is knowing the difficult crowd types and learning how to manage yourself with them.

THE CONTENT-DEFICIENT CROWD

The first type of difficult crowd suffers from content deficiency. They make unreasonable demands because they have low levels of information, trust, or access to their leader. You need to understand their frame of reference. They're not fully informed or engaged, and they feel victimized. Their leader has not been sharing context and building up shared knowledge.

This group requires listening and a lot of context. Bring them up to date with what's going on. Test, challenge, probe, and figure out what the etiology of their victimization is. You can't let their hopeless pessimism drain your energy or stir you in ineffective maneuvers. This may be a group that heard they're going to receive pay cuts, and they're very unhappy, but they didn't catch all the details or the plan for the upcoming year. They're kind of globally unhappy, but their unhappiness is not based on solid knowledge.

When an individual expresses a point of view that seems ill-informed or harmful in intent, the first step is to clearly understand their frame of reference...i.e., what makes their view rational to them?

—DR. BILL MARSH

The content-deficient crowd needs a lot of context to bring them up to date because their leader hasn't been doing his job. As a matter of fact, sometimes their leader is in the room with you and this difficult, content-deficient crowd will reference you in the third person, repositioning blame so it falls on you instead of them. Listen and be prepared for this to happen so you can address the crowd properly with the information they need.

THE HOSTILE MINORITY

The hostile minority is the 10 percent of a group attempting to dominate the discussion and take over the content. This crowd encompasses self-centeredness in the disagreements. Sometimes, their disagreements can be with the facts, your interpretation of the facts, or with your proposed actions. Their disagreements could be due to their general unhappiness or be based on something specific that happened to them. Sometimes the angriest person in the room used to be the chief and has been replaced—everything is personal after that. Managing this group is a core competency of an effective leader because a single voice can turn the meeting into a spectator sport.

Sometimes people in the hostile minority behave the same way, month after month. They talk to their CEO one month, and they talk to the hospital CFO the next month, and the nursing leader after that. The people with litanies of complaints feel as though they require a podium to voice their angst on a continual basis. These people want to use the room to voice their angst and animus. They're usually well-known to the audience, and they want to hijack your meeting.

Mud-wrestling with people like this degrades you. The rest of the people in the crowd want you to respect the hostile minority as long as you should, acknowledge what they say, challenge it, and give it back to them. Then ask, "Is this the common point of view? I have not heard this with such intensity before."

THE HOSTILE MAJORITY

This is the crowd you encounter when you walk into the room and most of the people are unhappy. They're outspoken, righteous, and feel betrayed by your leadership and that of others.

The situationally hostile majority, however, feels wronged.

These can be highly functioning professionals who have lost respect for their leadership, and they need to vent. It's your job to listen, acknowledge their thoughts, challenge them, and sort out how you arrived there. Again, pay attention to cynics versus dissenters. Perhaps they're unhappy about a tyrannical leader, or there's been an exodus of their excellent colleagues. Either way, they're not fools, and they're looking for capable leadership. You can't simply delegate this to someone else. They're looking for people to invest in them who care as much about their issues as they do. You must have a cool hand, be a good listener, and possess the humility to learn and the patience and tenacity to stay with the complexity and challenge. The situationally hostile majority is looking for engagement.

TOUGH CROWD PRINCIPLES FOR THE PHYSICIAN LEADER

Expect dissent. That's the first principle. Tough crowds are the norm. If you don't have a difficult crowd, you need to spend some time probing.

Number two, understand the intense issues. Don't go into a difficult meeting without at least talking to the chief—the leader of the group—or a trusted confidant (sometimes the problem is the chief). Get an idea of what people might throw in your face at the meeting. Understand the emotions involved. Wrap your mind around why people in the crowd will be difficult or hostile.

Third, honor their concerns; otherwise, you'll send the message that you're the boss, you're in charge, and people can only talk about what you want to discuss.

If the doctors expect to talk about a topic that's very important to them, such as the upcoming compensation plan, but you have hot-issue knowledge—for example, a change in Medicare—that needs to be addressed right away, let them know that up front. Say, "I set up this meeting a month ago to talk about some of the changes in the compensation system for next year, but as we all know, this is a pressing issue. I'd like to address all of your fears and concerns so that I can represent all of us when we have this conversation, and then we'll get back to compensation later if we have time."

Finally, it's necessary to maintain your leadership presence. Regardless of the size of the group, there will likely be people who try to dominate the conversation. It varies from people simply being interested, to disruptive and destructive.

On occasion, it can be useful to compare the reality of one group with that of another to provide context, but only if you do not do so out of spite. For example, if the primary care doctors are unhappy about their call schedules, you can remind them that the surgeons must work at the new hospital every other night. You're not trying to irritate these people or demean their issues; you are trying to work with them, and sometimes providing a view of the bigger picture gives them a perspective that you have and they do not.

Don't crumble, fall apart, or shrink from the conflicts. Don't beat them back by attacking them. Don't commiserate or confabulate with their despair, either, or come up with an unrealistic solution to calm them. Don't try too hard to rally them into seeing the world positively.

THREE WAYS TO SAY NO

Sometimes when you face a difficult crowd, you have to say no. You must let people know they are not going to get what they want.

Leaders have to say no in many situations in which their constituents or other leaders want them to say yes. You should be as transparent as possible about all the issues at hand and their reaction to the issues. Being a leader is not about being omniscient. It's about being courageous in the quest for answers.

There are three ways to say no.

1. HELL NO!

Sometimes you have to draw a hard line, such as when you're facing a state law. That's not even a simple no—it's a "Hell no." This is an emergency—a violation of the law— in which safety, ethical, or value issues are challenged. For example, Medicare has certain rules by which we must abide, and it's useless debating a topic we cannot control. "Hell no" means we can no longer do this.

2. WE AGREE TO DISAGREE

Communicate that your answer is no but that you're willing to try a different approach.

In this scenario, you've decided that despite their dissent, you want to move forward. However, you're willing to convene a small group to study the situation further. Depending on the urgency of the implementation, you can propose either a slow-start schedule or defer the decision for sixty days and put people from combined groups together to try to find a solution one more time. You welcome more input and declare you may change it later, but the answer is currently no.

3. I'VE HEARD ENOUGH BUT WILL MONITOR CLOSELY

Sometimes you say no and are also not planning on asking for more input from the group. You do commit, however, to measure and monitor the results for ongoing review. Here, you recognize that some people are still unhappy, but you've heard enough, you must decide, so you act to move forward.

Hold on to your position. Move ahead, measure the results, continue to monitor and learn, and promise to report back in a specific time frame with your findings and any modifications. Acknowledge that you respect them, but you do not require any more input at this stage, and your answer remains no.

The difference between the second and third option is nuanced. The second scenario is a bit more inclusive: you want to provide learning as you go, but you must move forward. The third one requires more decisive action.

The blowback from saying no, any no, can be so intense that you enter a war of wills, but you have to be a strong enough leader to make a decision and say, "This is my job. You will know whether I was right or not over time, as will I."

This is the core day-to-day reality of leading change in challenging times. Leaders must do this, and effective leaders get very good at this and become adept at managing themselves.

CHAPTER 8

PERFORMANCE MANAGEMENT

> ### ❓ WICKED QUESTION
>
> Do you have physicians in your group to whom you won't refer family members and friends?

There is great focus and interest in measuring and improving quality of care for patients and, as physicians, we consider it our responsibility and goal to always provide excellent quality of care to our patients. This commitment has created a need to understand how to be certain we know the level of quality provided and has resulted in developing an extensive science of measurement and an industry devoted to quality improvement. We understand that reliable, strategic processes for measurement are key to initiating the proper focus in learning about improvement science and developing improvement cultures in our hospitals, clinics, groups, and so on. While I introduce this topic under the heading of clinical quality, I remind us that the true physician as leader also accepts responsibility and leadership in other issues impacting patients such as service, access, equity, and affordability, as these are also components of the patient's experience in health care.

Depending on the structure and governance of the entity that is delivering the care, there can be a variety of professionals involved in quality measurement and improvement. And while any organization dedicated to quality improvement is well served to have a diversely capable group who oversee the quality measurement and improvement process, I will again focus on the physician role. This can be challenging work because we are measuring the work of people and colleagues whom we know well and often personally.

In any organized delivery system (hospital, clinic, medical group, etc.) there are basic requirements for being granted the right and privilege to practice there. These include specified educational and training preparation and board certification for general credentialing. Then for more specific scope of practice, the process of granting specific privileges occurs with some interval regularity to ensure the practitioner is maintaining a safe practice.

THE DILEMMA OF REVIEWING PEERS

A well-respected OB/GYN physician at a local hospital accepted the role and responsibility as chief of that service as part of his voluntary medical staff responsibilities. When he began doing the work, he realized there was some real discomfort with both the work and the findings. When he was asked to review some fetal monitoring tracings, he could clearly spot significant events of concern and opine on how to respond as a clinician. The hard part was the realization there could be patterns of concern involving individual colleagues' care. His stark realization was that, in this hospital, there were three types of OB/GYN doctors as he experienced them personally: partners, friends, and competitors. His relationships with these people could be significantly impacted by the physician simply doing his job. He emphasized how uncomfortable he was in evaluating any of these people because of these important relationships in his personal life.

When we began introducing performance management within the medical community, doctors were not disciplining doctors easily, readily, or often. At the hospital level, where the hospital oversaw management, you had to comply to keep your privileges. However, we weren't managing it as well within the community of medicine.

He said, "I really hated doing this and eventually was glad to finish my term. I was also glad the hospital had professionals to step in once the first issues were identified." I asked him, "Who should care if patients are being harmed?" and he said, "Obviously we all should." Then I named all who are affected by poor outcomes, including the low performer, and he really saw that as a difficult but very responsible and humane commitment to his peers. These are very tough issues, but physicians need to be central to setting standards, measuring, and creating performance improvement capabilities and culture.

So now we have this wicked question because we often know so much about our colleagues with or without the benefit of formal performance data. Do you have physicians in your group to whom you won't refer family members and friends? In other words, do you actively protect people you know and care about from seeing that doctor? One would hope the answer is no. When you personalize it by asking, "Have you ever said to your husband, 'Go see Dr. Smith, but don't see this one specific doctor,'" people often respond, "Oh, yeah, I do know someone like that."

This is the wickedest of the wicked questions because when you examine and measure physicians' performances, you potentially start to tamper with the lives, careers, and families of people. On the other hand, if you don't deal with low performers, you turn your back on them and their patients because most people don't transition from low performers to satisfactory or high performers spontaneously.

From Hertling's *Growing Physician Leaders*:

> All physicians, when discussing their profession in candid conversation, will admit to knowing one or two doctors who are allowed to "get away with" violations of medical standards. Substandard behavior by those with high volume/ high cost practices, or who might garner administrative

favoritism for some other reason, is sometimes excused. Doctors often dissemble when they face the requirement to discipline their own or to hold fellow physicians to professional standards. "Hey, I don't want to affect his lifestyle or his income," goes the frequent reply. But if physicians truly want to lead their profession—and I'm quite certain that most do—then they absolutely must make these hard calls. They have to determine which fellow professionals they need to discipline, hold accountable, and even dismiss, if necessary.[1]

WHY YOU SHOULD CARE AND ACT ON BEHALF OF PATIENTS AND OTHER COLLEAGUES

Most of us know a low performer, somebody we wouldn't send our family to. Physicians have problems. Errors are made. The data suggests that in a professional organization, 5 percent of your people have a problem, whether it's clinical quality, relationships, substance abuse, or some sort of emotional problem. Five percent is a societal reality, and we are part of this.

When I became president of our medical group, I went to my board of directors to introduce that while we were responsible for supporting and developing 600 doctors, we also directly cared for 400,000 patients. I had to ask

---

1   Mark Hertling, *Growing Physician Leaders: Empowering Doctors to Improve Our Healthcare* (New York: RosettaBooks, 2016), 41.

myself if there was a doctor I would protect my family from, and I said yes. I do direct family at times because of concerns. Reminder: this is extremely rare as we serve these patients day in and day out with proven and recognized superior quality.

There's another side of this equation, though. As the board of directors began to examine the issues of performance with an eye toward management and improvement, it became obvious that we had limited record keeping and often poor documentation regarding personnel files. In fact, many of the files, even for people being reviewed for performance concerns, appeared to be Lake Wobegon evaluations where the physician's abilities were likely overestimated.

Based on these findings, we had no basis to say we had done anything resembling due diligence or fair process. We had let this doctor bob along with this vague uneasiness about his performance. That methodology will cost you dearly because he could come back and say, based on his evaluations, he has done nothing wrong. Besides that, we had not given him the gift of continuous feedback over time. Performance management and performance improvement are not designed to discipline or harm. They're designed to measure and improve and can thus be humane and constructive toward the physician who is struggling.

Medical errors are the third leading cause of death in health care. If we decide to do nothing except protect our own family, then every fifteen minutes, somebody else's family member goes into the low performer's exam room, or every two hours, somebody else's family goes into a low performer's operating room because that doctor is still here. As a physician leader, protecting only the people you know and love, your family, is not enough.

Again, we are a highly autonomous profession. We have a legacy of rigorous, measured preparation, examination, and certification. We must prove ourselves multiple times, from premed, med school, and residency to certification, specialty boards, and hospital credentialing. We prove ourselves multiple times, and not in a vacuum. Once established, that intense scrutiny is understandably and appropriately less needed, but some system of measuring and monitoring and improvement is still essential. Obvious and extreme errors were readily discovered and addressed, but a more systematic process is essential to move beyond responding to these unusual problems.

Our medical group was self-governed and delivered care at the hospital but also at multiple outpatient clinics where there were hundreds of thousands of patient encounters each year.

I said to my board and leadership team, "How do we

define our role and responsibility?" We were part of the process of setting standards, measuring, and improving, but our system was still not identifying some issues that we were concerned about. But if we protect our families, we must decide who cares about patients who are not our families. The hospitals do. Patients and their lawyers do. The nurses do. If we're not willing to take a stand and set a bar, it says a lot to all those other groups.

The board of directors decided we should develop our own standards and expectations for each other in this professional corporation. In this thinking, we decided that we should care about clinical care and quality, but we should also look at behavioral issues such as teamwork, how we treat nurses, and how we treat patients. Five percent are fallen angels, and sometimes their job is the one thing they're hanging on to. Often, that person is in the exam room next door to us and is also the one closest to clinical issues and patients.

FOUR GROUPS SUFFER WHEN YOU DO NOT MONITOR, MEASURE, AND ACT

The responsibility of performance management is not something we as physicians necessarily signed up for. We did not sign up to look peers in the eye because we know how many standards they had to meet to get to where they are, and we are also aware of how hard it is for all of us in our own practices to always obtain ideal outcomes with our patients. But if a physician is performing on a low level of clinical quality or being a bad citizen, four groups suffer.

1. The patient suffers because they don't receive the best care. While this is obvious and our primary focus, the effect of harm goes well beyond the patient.
2. The other members of the team, such as nurses, suffer. They try to set a standard and a low performer drags them down. Remember, physicians have a disproportional impact. If the nurses and other doctors try to make improvements and I hold the bar down, I harm my team.
3. The third group that suffers from a lack of a performance management process is the high performers because they have to fix the problems. They take care of the angry patients and the complicated patients. That's an unpleasant job for the high performer.
4. The fourth group that suffers consists of the low performers themselves. No physician wakes up in the morning and says, "I think I'll do less than my best today." Everyone comes in well prepared, having gone through an amazing number of stages to succeed. The expectation is to do well; actually, it's to offer almost perfect care and perfect results. But if we do nothing to address those low performers, they will rarely spontaneously diagnose and correct themselves.

Some believe that our job as physician leaders is to protect and be protected by our fellow physicians—that it is part of the honor of the profession. There are enough rascals out to harm us, so we need to take care of ourselves. That's true in some areas, but not if patients are being harmed by the actions of people within our group.

Again, it goes back to the crux. If you believe people want to do well, but you don't help them, you shortchange them. I call it the humanity of performance management of your peers. Somebody has to care enough to say, "Jack, I've got to talk to you. I just want to tell you what I'm observing, what I'm seeing, and unfortunately, what I'm hearing." The reaction is not usually a positive one. Sometimes people thank you, but often, they say, "Baloney, my patients are more difficult than that doctor's, and you have had your share of complications also."

You hear a variety of answers, which is why you don't address this in isolation. You must create standards and expectations, systems of measurement, plans for professional development, support, and improvement, and then progressive evaluations. It must be done systematically, objectively, and fairly. You set up systems where people are more likely to succeed than fail.

CREATE A FORMAL PROCESS

In communicating my concern about doctors' performances with the board of directors, I acknowledged that everyone believed we had a small number of physicians who we wouldn't permit our families to see. No names were spoken. That wasn't the point of the meeting. The point was to answer the question, "What do we do?"

First, we had to formalize the process. You can't just wing performance management when you think someone needs help. Physicians need to know an evaluation and performance management process exists, so no one doctor feels like they're being singled out. Once, we had a fifty-five-year-old doctor come to work for the medical group. He was a recognized superstar of his specialty in the community. After ninety days, a thirty-five-year-old chief talked to him about his performance. "I didn't even want to talk to this person. I was a doctor before they were in high school," the older doctor said.

Performance management is difficult. You mess with the professional careers, reputations, and both the professional and personal lives of these people. You start to get to the core of their worth, their value, their identity, and their contribution. This is heavy duty. You can't discipline someone if you don't have evaluations, an evaluation process, and a comprehensive process to facilitate an improvement program tailored to the improvement issues of the individual.

You begin by figuring out the standards and what you believe you should measure, and this process needs to be open and the findings need to be transparent.

In this instance, I was president of the medical group and a member of the board. I told the board that these standards should be relatively simple. Let's not make it one hundred pages long. We're here to screen and find opportunities to endorse people or opportunities to make improvements. After our meeting, the board worked with human resources to set the standards. It began with a code of conduct, and then we focused on our values and the expectations of ourselves and of each other.

The code of conduct included standards such as a demonstrated commitment to our patients, practices, and one another; providing high quality, responsible medical care in a professional manner; interacting with other physicians, practitioners, staff, and leadership in a professional manner; and so on.

Once we agreed to these standards for measurement, we presented our analysis to the six hundred doctors, explaining that we did not have a way of monitoring performance and needed to for the sake of accountability. Not everyone thought this was a brilliant idea, but most people believed they were doing well, so monitoring their performance would not affect them. However, I'm sure some doctors saw it as possibly concerning since we weren't used to someone outside our clinical department having these measurements and recommendations.

Based on the code of conduct and measurement standards, we set up a simple evaluation process with some very crucial features. We had a set of questions to evaluate the doctor, the evaluation itself, and the evaluator. Evaluating the evaluator was key and not an initial idea. We didn't want an evaluator to dismiss the process by absentmindedly giving everyone high marks. We committed to the process for one year as a dry run and did not act upon our findings as we were learning how to do it right.

When some of the evaluations returned, a few people on the board were concerned about not acting when data about a low performer was staring us in the face. The low performers were smart people. They were well trained; they just weren't currently living up to the standards. Most, if not everyone on the board, knew in their hearts that these doctors were having some problems that were affecting their practice and patients.

The board believed we had to take action.

I maintained that we had assured physicians who participated in the evaluations that we wouldn't take disciplinary action based on the results. They wouldn't fire the low performers, but these doctors would enter a more detailed process of evaluation. The board promised to bend over backward to provide the low performers with the training, support, and education to get their evaluations to acceptable. At that point, some physicians may prefer to move on. Some people on the board believed the low performers wouldn't want to go through the process, but most did. The best outcome of a performance improvement program is improved performances. Not all did, not all could, and not all would or even wanted to, but most did improve.

Improved performance is the desired outcome and what I describe to people who don't want to implement a performance management program.

HOW TO BUILD YOUR OWN PROCESS

To begin a performance management program, there must be clarity on what is the accountable governing body and its relationship to the organization, leadership, and physicians. This accountable group, often a combination of the board of directors and leadership teams, must have direct oversight of all processes and decisions. Work with the board and partake in the iterative process to determine your core values. Core values generally revolve around good citizenship and high quality. Make them definite and true, state them with clarity, and chisel them in stone. This process of self-definition for the organization provides direction and guidelines to decide what are the important measures to develop to ensure you are measuring the right parameters and can act on the results.

This is how organizations build culture. When you recruit a new employee, you make your values and expectations clear and incorporate them into the recruitment process. You show new hires the same values and expectations in orientation, and they should recognize and understand them. When you provide training and development, you filter in the values and expectations, and finally, they are also part of the evaluation process. We'll discuss this further in chapter 10, "Culture." When you evaluate people for promotion, you refer to the organization's clearly defined and communicated values and expectations. Again, create clarity and be consistent. If you do that, people understand the values and expectations of the organization, and the culture development cycle works. Some won't like or abide by them, but most will.

INITIATING A PERFORMANCE IMPROVEMENT PLAN

1. Clarify governance and leadership roles and responsibilities

2. Confirm values and expectations
   a. Code of conduct
   b. Values and expectations

3. Develop measures to evaluate performance according to values and expectations

4. Initiate the evaluation measurements and evaluate the evaluators

5. Review initial round of evaluations to understand performance and learn about the process itself

6. Build performance improvement capabilities to support the needs and findings

7. Add a mechanism to track and evaluate the improvement programs being used

8. Determine the proper follow-up from the improvement program to track individual improvement

9. Continue this tracking with a transparent review of the total program

During this process, you must communicate the values, expectations, code of conduct, and performance management plan, and their places in your organizational culture, to all the peer groups, because if you've never done measurement before, the atmosphere will be tense, especially for the low performers, who will be on alert. Communicate the connection between the evaluations and the goal of building a healthy culture that benefits everyone.

Then, create the evaluation tools. You can use off-the-shelf tools or create your own simple, straightforward ones. Evaluations should include measurements that support the values of the organization and clearly identify what people are doing well and where they are lacking.

⚡ VOLTAGE DROP

A potential violation of the pristine process, aligned with clear values and expectations, is when an exception is inconsistent with the process that was sincerely developed and that won respect the hard way. This is when a decision is made to not discipline a physician because they are such a high producer or have such specific expertise. Allowing the exceptions sends clear messages throughout the future that there are two standards of belief.

When you review the evaluations, you'll discover some findings you don't like. Identify resources to support the low performers and have them in place. For example, in Colorado, the Colorado Physicians Health Program assists doctors with emotional, behavioral, and mental health stressors. The Colorado Physicians Education Program (CPEP) helps people who have lost their content by providing renewal or an update on their knowledge. If I went back to clinical practice, I'd go to CPEP and request a six-month refresher on plastic surgery.

The iterative process entails communicating to all the doctors to build trust. Town halls are important because you hear from people who don't want you to measure certain components of their work. On the other hand, some people like the performance evaluation, especially if they're high performers. They want their ambitious standards recognized. During the town halls, you get their input and gain credibility.

The town hall is somewhat of a metaphor. There are many types of gatherings and meetings. The point is that communicating the plan is not a one-time occurrence. When you talk about major change, you better have plenty of communication on what you're doing and why.

THE ROLE OF LEADERSHIP IN PERFORMANCE MANAGEMENT

Let's review and reaffirm the leadership expectations—being a respected clinician with integrity, emotional intelligence, humility, and passion—and the five C's of leadership: clarity, consistency, collaboration, compassion, and courage.

These expectations and traits are not esoteric, weird, or extensive. They're the qualities physician healers, leaders, and partners believe in and hold one another accountable to. Remember, it's about momentum, not speed. Go slowly with your board and other leaders to show them you're willing to learn and progress. If they are not willing to allow you to proceed, you must have the courage to ask them, "You think we should not measure performance? If we know someone is harming patients, we should do nothing?" Play that question back to them, because if one of us is harming patients, somebody will do something about it, whether it's the hospital or the lawyers. These physicians are our colleagues and friends, and even though it's tough to do interventions that impact their lives, in the long run, the most humane act is for us to care and act, but not protect them if they're harming people.

If your system works well and you commit to evaluating everyone once a year, you will find that after a year or two, the clear majority of people are superior. You never stop evaluating people, but in cases of year-after-year excellence, you evaluate them every other year or every third year. The people who are in flux or in improvement plans can be reevaluated in six months if necessary.

ADDRESSING THE LOW PERFORMER

Even physicians who have nothing to worry about will be concerned about their initial evaluation results. That's why there's an art to interventions. It takes skill to calmly and clearly communicate why and how someone could improve without making them feel insecure and assure them of your commitment to help them to continue performing at a higher level and have a distinguished career.

Once you have the evaluation results, identify the gaps and resources needed to fill in those gaps. Then you can construct a plan, which singles out specific steps that leadership, HR, and outside support systems, such as the local medical society, have in place. The plan should have tangible steps as well as a timeline. Reevaluate in ninety days, or the agreed-upon interval, and continue to monitor gaps. Occasionally, you must take immediate action. If there is evidence of criminal activity or major harm to patients, an urgent intervention is needed, supported by full disclosure to the board of directors with their continuous monitoring and approval and counsel. Proceed with great care and discipline.

Some people who perform badly may just be jerks, but that's a pretty minor group. When they are confronted with their evaluation results, they will test you, threaten you, and do everything possible to make your life miserable.

Most low performers are not within this group. Surround these people with support and opportunities to improve and give them every chance to succeed. After we initiated a performance management plan, it took about a year or two for the concerns in the medical group to lessen, when people realized they were getting good, reaffirming evaluations.

IT'S THE HUMANE THING TO DO

Assisting the low performer is the most humane thing you can do. It's the most caring thing you can do for another person, particularly because they aren't doing it themselves, or can't do it themselves. They don't want to cause harm, and you owe it to this person to listen to them and help them, even if it makes you uncomfortable. Again, failing to deal with low performers affects patients, families, team members, high performers, and the low performer.

Upon hearing their results of a performance review, the first reaction of a low performer is often not good, and a small number will be in denial. Although addressing the issue is the humane thing to do, it's not easy. When you're face-to-face with somebody and your kids play soccer together, or you know their spouse or that they have three tuition payments due, it's incredibly uncomfortable to speak to them about what they're doing wrong. Remind yourself that failure to deal with the issue only delays the opportunity to improve.

Your job is to communicate how some of their actions harm patients and how they can improve. Don't expect them to be immediately grateful, and in fact, you may get some blowback. A low performer you seek to counsel might claim you're simply out to get them. Listen to their concerns. Explain that your goal is not to be punitive but to help them improve. Discuss possible next steps, such as additional training or education and possibly some level of monitoring or restrictions on what they're allowed to do. You may be surprised to find that some physicians have simply reached their limit and are prepared to retire rather than continue with the process.

I cannot emphasize enough here that, even though assisting the low performer is the humane thing to do, they may not see it that way and may in fact be in a very unstable frame of mind. Never underestimate how traumatic this experience may be for the individual. Your actions have the potential to adversely affect their career, their family, and their reputation. They may react very badly, even violently, toward you, others, or themselves. For this reason, it is imperative that the intervention be followed immediately with a plan for moving forward.

Performance management is not about making people

feel nervous or inadequate, or about firing people. The best and most humane outcome of measuring performance is improvement.

DEALING WITH THE LOW PERFORMER EFFECTIVELY

After you do an evaluation and come to your results, create a performance improvement plan supported by evidence. Put the plan in place, integrate the support, and then detail your recommendations and the conditions for moving forward. Listen and understand but remain resolute. Do not compromise but promise to be supportive. You must show due process and illustrate how it's carried out impartially with adherence to standards that were agreed upon and published by the governing body for the group or clinical facility.

When you first start this process, the reactions of the physicians being evaluated are all over the board. However, once people see that it works, the value is often recognized. Your high performers will thank you because you have endorsed their outstanding performance and relieved them of the burden of concern for the patients and staff working with a low performer.

Initially, this work is rarely viewed as a positive by performers who know they need to improve, but fortunately, when you first start the process, you have a lot more in the pipeline that's negative than you have after five years of doing it. It is very gratifying to see the tangible improvement in the practice and the life of a colleague who was having problems and to know that the overall impact on care and culture is very positive.

While you are executing your plan, have a progressive discipline where everything is documented, and it will quickly become clear that you're doing the right thing. The ethos of the medical group over time develops into pride of this process.

When the evaluation process was initiated, a small number of individuals made their own decision to pursue a different future. We didn't have an internal lawyer, but we had a lawyer on speed dial because we were dealing with people's livelihoods and reputations, and we didn't want to violate their well-being. We found that, sometimes, low performers had been taking on harder patients, and they realized they needed to stop doing that. Those who didn't make it were given an objective process based on public standards and a program to promote improvement and support throughout the process.

Some individuals who were involved in their performance improvement program for a few months weren't confident more time and observation would result in the desired outcome and improvements, so they decided to leave. Some completely left the practice of medicine and found other satisfying work and careers. While I hate to see these transitions in people who had worked hard and been devoted to the profession, the process was fair and humane.

Most of the people who left didn't thank us. One person who left was quite popular, and some of his friends sort of threatened me. Our process and communication were completely private, completely secure, and completely silent, but despite my playing by the rules, this person told everyone I fired him.

Notably, within a year and a half, two of his friends privately and discreetly told me I did the right thing.

A TALE OF TWO INTERNISTS

Two physicians, Charlie and Jake, both in their fifties, worked side by side in a community hospital. They were competitors, as they weren't in the same practice, but they were friendly and respected one another, as they were both great doctors. People considered them deans of their specialty. Charlie left his practice to work with our medical group in our local clinic. They remained close friends, though Jake was still in private practice. After working with us for six months, Charlie had an appointment with his chief, who showed him the data on his performance. The chief was a young, brilliant, thirty-five-year-old woman telling this fifty-two-year-old man how he needed to improve.

Charlie said, "I know my results. I'm doing an excellent job. Who are you to be measuring me? You were in junior high school when I was in medical school."

She told him he indeed does an excellent job most of the time, but there were gaps and deficiencies in his performance. Because we measure them in our system, they were obvious. In the end, Charlie was grateful his chief convinced him of where he needed to improve and provided him with the proven internal support—from nursing, pharmacy, online tools, other physicians, and medical education—that made it easy for him to enhance the quality of care for his patients.

He said, "It was an interesting process for me because I knew I was a good doctor. Then they showed me the results. I think I'm still a good doctor, but obviously I have some significant gaps in quality of care that I need to close."

He did that and, six months later, he received his results. They were significantly better.

Charlie ran into his old friend at a medical meeting.

Jake, who still worked in private practice, said to him, "I don't understand all this evaluation and performance management stuff, Charlie. You and I both know we're great doctors. We've always been great. We're the best doctors in this community, and we've been that way for thirty years."

Charlie's response was, "You know, Jake, you're right. You might be the best doctor I've ever known. But I'm now positive that I'm a great doctor because I have proof. I have measurements. When I say I'm doing an excellent job, I can say to you, 'Jake, you ought to see my results.'" He explained that the culture of measurement was wonderful once you got past the indignation of someone measuring you.

Jake was a little confounded, but it was a wonderful moment.

Performance management of individuals shows respect and responsibility toward the patient and other affected members of the health care team. It also shows humane compassion and commitment for the low performer.

PART III

PHYSICIAN AS PARTNER

The role of healer is central to the trusted one-on-one relationship between physicians and patients. The role of leader is important to ensure that a strong clinical voice is present in decisions and strategies deployed in organizations of all kinds and structures. Physicians who opt in can be strong advocates for patients.

However, as the issues in health care have become more and more complex, meaningful participation requires collaboration and functioning through influence within groups and teams. Examples of these include: selection and deployment of IT systems, debates on strategy and operations, allocations and prioritization of budgets, and even the management of multiple complex patients whose care requires many inputs. To be optimally effective in these challenging group environments, physicians must define and enhance the role of physician as partner.

CHAPTER 9

LEADING CHANGE

❓ WICKED QUESTION

Why is the established science of human motivation and behavior overlooked in corporate culture development?

No one writes books on leading the status quo. Leadership requires leading change. All of us continuously face the corporate and personal challenges of changing business environments, challenging competition, and need for improvement.

When physicians are checked out, frustrated, and preoccupied, it is not easy to motivate them to make major, innovative, or transformative changes. Conversely, I see groups and systems where physicians are engaged, enthused, well-prepared, and well-supported. They are formidable agents for change.

We hear these sentiments a lot: "You know, we'd like to do it, but the doctors don't want to, or the doctors are opposed to that." At times, doctors get compartmentalized and labeled as people who are over there, and they don't quite get it, and they don't collaborate as much as we'd like them to.

We have myriad methodologies and theories for leading change, but often, those methods emphasize the what and the how, rather than the why. We don't invest enough in the why behind the importance of leading change.

Unfortunately, what we define as change, others might define as loss. Leaders frequently get so personally focused on the need for the proposed change that they underinvest in communication, discussion, and getting the targets for the change adequately informed, prepared, supported, and engaged. It takes time to explain why the change is necessary, and to entertain legitimate questions and concerns. It might not affect everyone in the room, but it matters. Even for a change as obviously positive as a new IT system, its newness means it will be disruptive, making people wary of the process and impact. Personal motivation is key, because you're working with a group of professionals. You're not just trying to create onerous change in their lives and make them behave; you're trying to have them, ideally, be enthused and eager to make improvements. That's where you get discretionary effort.

For example, I once walked into a room of unhappy orthopedic surgeons. They had been in the central hospital of Denver, St. Joseph, since they started. We were building a second hospital in the north part of the city and planning to move some people there.

Someone said, "You don't have to tell us. We know what you're up to."

As opposed to accepting this, it was vital to communicate that I understood their reality and asked them to understand mine. "We're actually moving to two hospitals," I explained, "one north and one south, over the next year, so that in a city growing as fast as Denver, we don't have to have everyone traveling forty or fifty miles to the central hospital. This is our first move."

Two people continued to complain—they did not want "to be told they had to go to the new hospital"—at which point I acknowledged their points of view and communicated mine.

"We have 400,000 members in the Denver area and, based on our analysis, about 160,000 of them will use the new north hospital, while 240,000 will stay at the central one. I need thirty-two orthopedists to take care of 400,000 people. Now, I need twelve orthopedics in the north hospital. It will be a full-service hospital. How do I get twelve people there if you won't go?"

I told them I could put an ad in the orthopedics journal and start hiring orthopedists, which would create some inconvenient mathematics for the current group. If we hired twelve new orthopedists, then we would have a significant overstaffing/distribution problem. I said it seemed clear to me that we would then need to deal with an overstaffing problem at the original, central hospital and couldn't rationalize keeping all thirty-two of this original group.

Suddenly, people began grumbling less and listening more.

One man said, "It's pretty obvious. We have to stop talking about this and start making plans." When another doctor asked what would happen if he didn't want to go, I explained that not all thirty-two of them had to leave, only twelve, and it didn't need to be any specific doctor. Nonetheless, I was overstaffed in orthopedics at one hospital, and they had to realize that presented a problem.

It was a complex, difficult evening involving a long

iterative discussion. I wasn't angry or rude. I listened, acknowledged, challenged, and kept framing the issue—including their interests—to solve the problems together.

INTRINSIC AND EXTRINSIC VALUE, DISCRETIONARY EFFORT AND CHANGE

Discretionary effort comes from engaging people on their personal values and mission. It can arise from intrinsic value.

Extrinsic value relates to how a leader can manipulate or convince a person to do something, perhaps with incentives. We try to motivate people to perform or do a certain behavior or engage in an activity to either get a reward or avoid a punishment. So it is, like the name says, driven by external forces, often money.

Again, refer to chapter 5 and McGregor's Theory X and Theory Y. Would a Theory X leader be more likely to rely on motivational techniques that rely on intrinsic or extrinsic value? What about a Theory Y leader?

Intrinsic value denotes deeply caring and having a sense of purpose in the action a person carries out. Intrinsic motivation is about engaging in behaviors because they're personally rewarding to individuals. They intrinsically want to change because it helps them in some way.

It makes them feel good. It's something they believe in. It's not about desiring an external reward.

Simon Sinek talks about this kind of extrinsic versus intrinsic motivation in his book *Start with Why*.[1] We have tried to develop the perfect extrinsic motivators for years in corporate America. Frankly, if we had arrived at those perfect motivators, they would be broadly accepted and we'd probably all be using them. We obviously don't have them figured out, though. On the other hand, scientific studies have consistently proven that intrinsic motivation encourages people to not only put in discretionary effort, but also to put their whole heart and soul into a project. They do more than simply what's necessary. They're not complacent with change, so they engage in finding even better ways to improve.

This is especially challenging for physicians. Based on the way in which they are trained to accurately diagnose and treat the medical model, they often focus on the *what* and the *how* for solutions. Getting physicians to shift their paradigm to see it from a perspective of why and then moving to a space of shared vision when you lead teams, is challenging. That's one of the biggest things you can do to tap into that intrinsic motivation. This sense of why

---

1   Simon Sinek, *Start with Why: How Great Leaders Inspire Everyone to Take Action*, (New York: Portfolio, 2009).

was clear to the twenty-one-year-old idealist hoping to become a healer and physician.

It's easy when you are twenty-one and filling out an application, teeming with idealism. You endure the what and the how and countless hours because your why is still focused on this incredibly selfless mission of serving and healing. That's why you don't have to talk a lot about why when you are twenty-one. Then the system starts to gnaw at you and the scales tilt a little bit. How can we learn to redefine, renew, and reboot our sense of personal mission? And as important, how can we transform the daily professional reality of physician practice that is no longer described with words like "survival" and "sustainability" to a new professional reality where the experience includes satisfaction, stimulation, optimism, and joy? Sinek might recognize this as rediscovering our why and improving the how to create a consistent what.

Organizations and the way we instill different policies and practices kill that why—that internal drive and discretionary effort—because of the crazy things we've put into place. Rules and policies can crush the soul and take all the autonomy out of the practice. Organizations are at the crux of so many of these elements. So, a physician who is twenty years into their practice might have lost some of the clarity and enthusiasm of why they're still doing what they're doing.

Then, someone affectionately referred to as a "suit" tells the physician they must improve productivity and efficiency and will do this by cutting FTEs (full-time employees), so they have to work smarter, not harder... and more clichés.

In *Drive: The Surprising Truth About What Motivates Us*,[2] Daniel Pink has culminated an abundance of research from the social sciences to obtain a better understanding of what's going on in order to heighten our thinking as it relates to motivation at work.

This ties into leading change because organizations are wired to believe that people are motivated by money, so they get people to change or do something different by paying them. A lot of this research has proven that belief to be false. So Pink describes two distinct kinds of work.

The technical phrase for the first kind of work is "algorithmic tasks." Those are tasks that follow a formula that exists today. They have a process we know how to get through, with start and end points. In the health care space, there are some algorithmic tasks for physicians— proven, reliable processes that need to happen, such as colonoscopies, appendectomies, cataract surgeries, etc.

---

2   Daniel H. Pink, *Drive: The Surprising Truth About What Motivates Us* (New York: Riverhead, 2011).

The other kind of work is "conceptual tasks," which demand some flexible problem-solving, inventiveness, and ingenuity. There isn't a clear process of how to get from point A to point B because one has done it well in the past. I see this as it relates to this discussion. Leaders try to lead a large organization that's a complex, adaptive system. They don't know how to shift humans most of the time, so they must step back and creatively determine how to get physicians to do X, Y, or Z.

Pink found that for those conceptual tasks, people have an inverse relationship with external rewards. This creates a massive challenge when organizations motivate people with incentive programs and bonuses because people perform inversely for these conceptual level tasks. According to his research, people perform worse when there are carrots dangling in front of their face.

In *Drive*, Pink argues further, if we are rethinking what it means to lead change in organizations, we have to get out of the Industrial Revolution mindset and come into this new knowledge age. What is it that people are driven by? It turns out his research would identify autonomy, mastery, and purpose as the three most important aspects to lead change. Autonomy is the desire to direct your own life and have a say in how you do things. Mastery is the desire to continually improve and learn. Purpose is being a part of something meaningful.

Leaders should then think beyond incentive plans and bonus plans and think through the lens of intrinsic motivation. For example, in approaching autonomy, give employees more freedom while maintaining clearer accountability. The opposite of that approach is being the micromanaging leader who kills autonomy in a heartbeat.

Lastly, purpose harkens back to the Simon Sinek "why conversation." Engage employees, engage your colleagues, determine why they do what they do, and help them see the connections—the overall purpose—and the why in their job.

These three elements are often missing in organizations. We see a lot of carrots and sticks, and when a person doesn't achieve a certain milestone, they get punished. This creates an organization that lacks soul, and the ability to be inventive, adaptable, and nimble. Engagement also plummets.

The United States Army has an interesting reflection on this in a surprisingly accurate parallel to health care. When they came out of Vietnam, they had a command-and-control culture. The soldier could be lying in the jungle, and the lieutenant ordered him around by walkie-talkie, and the soldier did as he was told. As the issues inherent in war and the knowledge around them became more complex, they realized this model didn't work the way it used to. They discussed changing these eighteen-year-olds from needing to respond to direct orders to becoming people who autonomously manage information and make decisions based on continuous updates of data. The technological change mirrors that of health care. Today's soldiers now have handheld smart devices, GPS devices on their wrists, and they manage data and information interpreted by algorithms and probability that are processed halfway around the world.

In *Hope Is Not a Method*, Generals Sullivan and Harper state the following.

> We are in a 'fertile verge...a place of encounter between something and something else.' We stand between a bureaucratic industrial society and an information society. The skills we have used all our lives are falling short of helping us face the new world; it is a time of fantastic opportunity but also of ambiguity and uncertainty. In times like this, management is not enough. Ours is a time for leadership.[3]

When I read this book, I thought the authors were speaking to me. Health care is behind the US Army, which, at that time, was becoming a more change-friendly organization. It was so striking to me that we have all those

3   Gordon R. Sullivan and Michael V. Harper, *Hope Is Not a Method: What Business Leaders Can Learn from America's Army* (New York: Broadway, 1997).

doctors who are much more advanced than an eighteen-year-old but are still being beaten up by a system that's changing without them.

⚡ VOLTAGE DROP

Leading major change requires attention to a large number of major issues and constituencies with a time constraint and with the challenge of managing the existing reality while deploying the new desired state. It tests the tension between short-term relief and long-term success. If you underinvest in communication, training, deployment support, and time for mastery, you are at great risk to end up with a less-than-adequate new state and culture enabled by the change you led.

One of the big stressors in life is having increasing demands without the autonomy to make the changes. I've seen this firsthand within health care organizations and physician leaders. When managers tell teams exactly how things need to be done, autonomy dies. The leader kills the individual's sense of competence and pride. This goes back to the conversation about Theory X and Theory Y. Do you believe the people working with you and for you are competent and will do what's in the best interest of the patient, or do you feel like you must tell them what to do and constantly monitor them? Giving them autonomy and trust allows them to say, "This is the outcome we need, and we will value your thoughts, opinions, and solutions. It does not mean we are lax on measuring outcomes and learning from variations both positive and negative. It does say that while we have some tasks for which we have proven formulae to solve, we are also a learning organization with a culture that leverages creativity and energy."

Trust.

The first step of leading change is showing up. For a massive disruptive change, it's not sufficient to send your director or VP. You, as leader, must stand up and say, "This is important to me, so I'm going to disrupt your lives and ask you to make changes, but I will also explain why we need to change." Then you listen to them, answer their questions, receive feedback, challenge them, and acknowledge them.

This takes an investment of time to inform, listen, challenge, and build shared understanding by cocreating context from which to discuss proposed solutions and changes. Without this, you miss discretionary nuanced feedback, enthusiasm, and criticism that you could use to shape an even better outcome. The change itself is rarely enough to excite people. That's the contrast between a brief memo and a true conversation.

Leadership, like communication, is a longitudinal commitment. It is important that you not only go to the group to share what the future looks like and what you think needs to be done, but also, to listen. Sometimes, through listening, you avoid problems you wouldn't have foreseen on your own. It goes back to credibility, which comes from both your ability to influence and your willingness to be influenced (listen and learn). Your knowledge base is different, and you often have facts or insights that the group has not heard or understood. You serve the group, so you try to influence them, but you listen as well because you believe in and want to understand the others' important views so you can fine-tune your plan and make course corrections in the implementation or deployment.

DEVELOPING A METHODOLOGY FOR LEADING CHANGE BY TRIAL, OBSERVATION, AND LEARNING

Much of what I know about leading change was learned by trial and error, enabled by initial inexperience. My inexperience kept me from developing a chip on my shoulder. I didn't believe I had to be more powerful, persuasive, manipulative, or charismatic to lead change. I realized that attitude would be a thin veneer, and instead, I had to learn to listen.

When I first began my career as a practicing surgeon, I had completed four years of medical school, six years of a surgical residency program, and a certification process. I had extensive training and verification of competence. When I became a leader in the business of medicine, most of my training was just in time, on the job, trial and error, and I was learning as quickly as I could. Preparing for that role followed a very different approach and process than my medical training. I didn't stop my life for three years, get an MBA, and then work a couple of midlevel development jobs to become a leader. It was so completely different than the depth and extent of training that you get as a physician, but I learned, nonetheless.

SENIOR LEADERS' PERSONAL REQUIREMENTS

In addition to a methodology for organizational change management to deploy major changes, senior leaders also must possess three traits to ensure that they are vigilant and don't miss important problems requiring change. These are awareness, humility, and courage.

Awareness is the discipline to understand that you always have areas of performance where you are deficient and that there are excellent solutions in place outside of your organization. General organizational success can produce good, aggregated results which are assuring. However, good aggregated results usually contain variation, including areas of poor performance, with challenges and deficiencies. You must be intentional in acknowledging these areas and intentional in your awareness of the cold reality and weaknesses that accompany them. That's not easy. When things are going well, you still have to say, "Which areas are not good enough? Where are the areas that I have got to continue to understand so we can make them significantly better?" That's awareness.

Humility is being able to admit to yourself and your colleagues that you don't have all the answers. Therefore, you seek learnings from a broad scan of organizations, people, information, and literature. Intellectual humility demands you concede to having challenges you didn't anticipate and a willingness to tackle them with the help of your team. Those who can honestly embrace intellectual humility are proven to be much better learners.

As leaders, we live and die in aggregate results. We care about quality scores, membership numbers, and income and profit margins, and these aggregate numbers are broad indicators of success. The issue is, aggregate numbers simply refer to an average, and within them you finally have some places where you're superior, but you've also got some real problem areas.

As leaders, that's where awareness and humility come in. Because we often focus on quarterly results, when the aggregate results come in, we breathe a big sigh of relief. It takes a little starch to recognize that we might have had a great quarter overall but that some aspects were terrible.

The third trait required to lead change effectively, after awareness and humility, is courage. Courage is turning to yourself and your organization, relating what you've learned, conveying the need for correction, and then delving into the process of listening, acknowledging, and challenging. And for those who have done this, we know it is not easy to face your own valued and trusted teams and leaders and relate that you have found a better solution in another organization. Even if the truth should be crucial, it still reflects on colleagues. The ideal is that the senior leader possesses all three of these traits.

Awareness, humility, and courage provide a base upon which to lead change. The following steps will move your team forward in the implementation.

METHODOLOGY FOR SUCCESSFUL CHANGE

I never went through any major change without immediately saying, "I better check the temperature of the
water. I better find the deep holes I'm going to fall into
and would never have anticipated." That's what your
team is there to warn you about, but in a professional
organization, there's nothing like showing up, telling
people what you think reality is like, and then getting their
feedback. Sometimes you get into very big, very serious
disagreements, but this is preferable to allowing them to
undermine you and destroy the process.

I've used one particular methodology on four occasions.

BUILDING SHARED CONTEXT AND COCREATING VISION

One component of this methodology is absolute clarity
of vision and goal. You can't create a major change where
your strategy is hope. There must be great intentionality
and great investment to make change work. This is disruptive, and again, while you may see it as change, many
will see it as loss. Take putting in an IT system. People will
worry about being embarrassed because they're usually
looking sharp in their clinical field, so the reaction will
be, "I don't need this. I want to get out of this." While
the methodology I will describe has been used in several
major change strategies, I will illustrate it in the deployment of a new clinical IT system across the entire region

because: (1) it truly impacted every physician, nurse, employee, and patient in the region; and (2) we had great time urgency to replace a weakened and aging existing system in a few weeks.

The first step of leading change is to stand up in front of your people and arrive at an iterative establishment of the issues. To ground a group of professionals in the need to make a major, disruptive change, it is essential for leaders to share information and context about why this difficult change is essential. This is not a single convincing speech or memorandum. Rather, it is about a commitment to an iterative communication journey of proposing, listening, reacting, and learning to cocreate and arrive at a shared understanding of why the changes are essential. Develop a sense of what the problem is, provide answers for why you need to make a change, and then—with some of their input—you can make the change with a decisive, clear path.

Once the vision is clear and the detailed preparation has been deployed, operational execution is the proof of the process.

BUILD CAPACITY FOR CHANGE BY PROVIDING TRAINING AND SUPPORT

The second step is making an adequate and intentional investment in training and support so individuals have the psychological and mental space for undistracted learning. This is where the change process frequently falls apart. I've watched people trying to learn new IT systems in tears. People will say they understand when they're really brushing you off, hoping to avoid humiliation. Don't start a new IT system in the middle of a doctor-patient relationship. You must support physicians up front with time, training, and people.

There must be commitment to provide extensive training in many formats. In addition to basic small group classes, which were highly interactive and produced a spirit of group learning, we also provided DVDs and online training in preparation for the change.

This new IT system implementation was required because the old legacy system was falling apart so fast that we were going to go back to paper records if we weren't careful. We had to get the legacy system out. We couldn't manage care easily with two systems running in parallel, so it was a situation where speed was important. We put in a complete, brand-new system for 400,000 patients, 600 doctors, 5,000 employees, and seventeen clinics in four weeks and two days. It was the land-speed record for IT implementation. We overstaffed on our IT support, technical support, and clinical replacement staff, and decreased schedules to a very low level.

I told my team that all six vice presidents and I would also receive training. Two of the VPs argued that they never saw patients and didn't require training. I said, "No. This is the biggest disruption that will probably happen in the region on our watch. We're going to get trained. We're going to be able to use this device. We won't be cocky and say we can solve all problems and expect people to learn this unless we show them we can learn it too."

We went through the online training, classroom training, and mentoring. I instructed us to spend all day in the clinics where the deployment was happening, and every day at noon, we had a two-hour team phone meeting to bring each other up to date on the IT deployment as well as to discuss the operational and financial issues in our day jobs. Our offices were empty for a large portion of those four and a half weeks.

I went to one of the clinics and watched my chief of surgical services talking to a woman who was new and entry level.

He said, "Hey, Joan, how are you doing?"

She said, "Oh, I'm doing great, Doctor. No problems. I like this system."

He said, "Would you mind showing me how you get

somebody's records from an outside hospital and put them into the record?"

She responded, "I'm not so sure we've gone over that yet."

He laughed and said, "Well, I couldn't figure it out. That task completely stumped me."

Then, he pulled up a chair and sat next to her. Her shoulders just relaxed. The doctor explained that he had trained on this system and, therefore, believed he knew it but was having difficulties. They walked through it together. I wish we had videotaped it. He gave her peace, her mind relaxed, and she opened up. It was such a great human act. The degree of support he provided allowed her to learn. When you do that, you get more discretionary effort, enthusiasm, and feedback.

Again, unless your CFO is tearing their hair out, you're not putting in enough support. If you lose money for a few months because you were overstaffed, that problem can be solved. If you put in a system that is not fully understood or fully deployed for years, you can't even measure what it's going to cost you—not to mention the ringer you put people through.

LEVERAGE THE ENTHUSIASM OF POSITIVE PEERS

It is imperative that the first group of users succeeds to a level that they will not only proudly and openly share their enthusiasm, but also become resources for the groups that follow. Don't start with people that are the most vitriolic and resistant to change. Find those people who say, "Me first, me first, me first." If 600 people need to accept the change, 580 people will want to know what the twenty who went first have to say.

That group might say, "This thing rocks. The first morning was crazy, but these people from the IT department helped us with the technical issues. We had other doctors seeing our patients, so we had the space to learn. By day two, we had it figured out, and were using the new system and seeing four patients in the morning and the afternoon."

We carefully identified a group of enthusiastic, capable early adopters in a midsized clinical facility and supported them with a team of: (a) clinicians to care for most of the patients while the users were training at a pace where they could excel; (b) onsite technical support people to provide real-time response for technical problems; (c) IT experts, initially experts from the IT organization but, at subsequent deployment sites, also included superusers from the first clinics; and (d) administrative support who were a small group of folks that were simply extra arms, legs, and eyes who improved deployment execution and were phased out over time. To optimize opportunities for getting off on the right foot, these carefully selected early adopters proved to be eager users and quick learners who acted as models for other clinics. These clinics produced the first superusers, who were added to the support team to go to subsequent clinics. The credibility of these peer clinician superusers created a real buzz in the region, and this helped develop the powerful trust that this was not just a leadership project, but a true advance and success in the eyes of peers. As subsequent clinics began to go live, experience created valuable learning, making the process even more effective.

That is the truth. Whatever you, as the leader, say is secondary to the street credibility and clinical credibility of one's peers. Let the early adopters be successful. Let them show the others what enthusiasm and change can look like. Speed comes from the resultant trust and then momentum. That's the trust curve.

🔑 KEY POINT

Speed does not come from going fast. It comes from momentum created through trust.

This is where the trust curve comes into play. Speed does not come from moving quickly; it comes from developing an organization with a keen ability for execution that creates trust. Speed comes from momentum. Develop a culture that embraces measurement, acknowledgment, improvement, and challenge, and you build a group skill-set of change management and improvement.

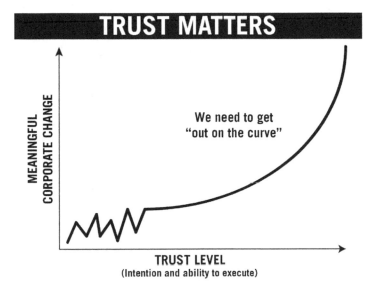

TRUST MATTERS

We need to get "out on the curve"

MEANINGFUL CORPORATE CHANGE

TRUST LEVEL
(Intention and ability to execute)

As I conveyed in the trust curve metaphor, there are two types of trust. One is the trust of intention, and the other is the ability to execute. If I don't trust your intention, we have a problem. However, trusting your intention isn't enough. You might be honorable and honest, but if you haven't come through in the past, then I don't trust your ability to execute.

BE CURIOUS, NOT FURIOUS

During the transition to the new IT system, I prepared people for the challenge ahead. I sent out voicemails, one of which said, "This is going to be hard. We're clinical leaders, nurses, and doctors, individually competent in our fields. You've proven yourselves. This deployment is going to expose that you're not as competent as you would hope to be, so it's going to be frustrating. There are going to be times when you think, 'I'm used to controlling my day, and here I am frustrated because things are not going well.' Because everyone is subjected to this, I ask that when you get frustrated, be curious, not furious."

By that I meant that the people with the green shirts on are technical support. The people with the yellow shirts on are IT support. The people with the orange shirts on are physician backups. Find them and get support. I then became known as the curious-not-furious man. They thought that was hysterical.

I was on the cardiology floor, and I ran into these two cardiologists who were just wickedly smart, capable, brilliant human beings. One of them said, "Oh, well, look who's here. Look who found a clinic. Did somebody show you a map to get you out to a clinic?" He continued, "You know, Jack, you should come over here because we are really, really getting curious. As a matter of fact, I've never seen Steve more curious. He's getting *so* curious."

I asked, "Really? How curious are you?"

He said, "Well, we're deciding which one of us is going to go over and open up the window and throw the computer out."

I told them we were on the twelfth floor, and that probably wasn't a very good idea. Besides that, I wasn't hearing curiosity. I was hearing fury.

They said, "You're a fast study, Cochran, because this system is a piece of crap."

But I had good news for them. I told them Andy Lum, who was on my team, was an IT genius, and he would sit down with them and help them understand. It took about an hour for Andy to have them up and running.

CHAPTER 10

CULTURE

❓ WICKED QUESTION

What is the impact of presenting a clear vision and set of expectations externally but then departing from them when it is expedient because the situation is urgent or difficult?

Central to the message of this book is the need for physician leadership and identifying the essential beliefs, skills, and behaviors needed to lead health care into the future. However, this message would be incomplete without a conversation about the role of culture in fostering the success of leaders and organizations as well as how it can derail success when not guided with purpose and intention.

Organizational culture, by its very nature, is often elusive and confounding for leaders. It is this nebulous, unseen, and intangible powerful force that drives behavior, shapes attitudes, impacts outcomes, and is a felt sense throughout an entire organization. Unfortunately, many leaders underestimate the power of culture and either let it go completely unmanaged or delegate it to one specific department to manage, such as human resources. Instead, these leaders spend their time laying out detailed strategic plans and objectives, driving to specific goals only to find this hard work completely derailed by the unspoken rules, beliefs, and ways of doing work. Like many have said before, culture eats strategy for breakfast.

So, what is culture? From the father of organizational culture, Edgar Schein:

> The culture of a group can now be defined as a pattern of shared basic assumptions learned by a group as it solved its problems of external adaption and internal integration, which has worked well enough to be considered valid and, therefore, to be taught to new members as the correct way to perceive, think, and feel in relation to those problems.[1]

I've come to know culture as, simply, the way we do things around here. It is the way we get work done, how we make decisions, how we collaborate, how we use authority

---

[1] Edgar H. Schein, *Organizational Culture and Leadership*, 4th ed. (San Francisco: Jossey-Bass, 2010).

and power, and how we recognize good work, to name a few. Several generally agreed upon characteristics help us better grasp the nature of culture. A recent *Harvard Business Review* article highlighted four specific attributes:

1. Shared. Culture is a group phenomenon. It resides in shared behaviors, values, and assumptions.
2. Pervasive. Culture is everywhere. It is manifest in collective behaviors, environments, group rituals, symbols, and stories.
3. Enduring. Culture can direct the thoughts and actions of group members over the long term. People are drawn to organizations with characteristics similar to their own. Culture becomes a self-reinforcing social pattern that grows increasingly resistant to change.
4. Implicit. Despite its subliminal nature, people are effectively hardwired to recognize and respond to it instinctively. It acts as a silent language.[2]

Whether we recognize it or not, culture becomes a critical ingredient to the success of the physician healer, leader, and partner, and it all begins with the crux. Clearly understanding one's beliefs, views, perspectives of their colleagues, and honest self-awareness are essential ingredients to building a healthy and strong culture.

---

2   Boris Groysberg, Jeremiah Lee, Jesse Price, and J. Yo-Jud Cheng, "The Leader's Guide to Corporate Culture," Harvard Business Review (January–February 2018), accessed February 10, 2018, https://hbr.org/2018/01/the-culture-factor#the-leaders-guide-to-corporate-culture.

Beliefs and practices rooted in manipulation, coercion, and force create a culture that reflects that very essence in results and outcomes—often limited sustainability and a team environment that is toxic to the soul of the human being. However, beliefs and practices rooted in trust, collaboration, accountability, and an inherent belief in the goodness of people result in great team environments where people feel connected, engaged, respected, and challenged, where they go above and beyond for their patients and colleagues, leading to sustained business success.

Leadership and culture are truly two sides of the same coin, inextricably linked to one another. The founders or top leaders in an organization, knowingly or not, set the foundation, tone, and values that drive the culture and operations for decades. Skilled leaders begin to understand how their beliefs, behaviors, and attitudes shape the dynamics around them. Similarly, the culture can also shape leaders. Once a culture is well established, the unwritten rules and norms influence how leaders behave, how they make decisions, how they posture themselves with colleagues, and how they show up for everyone else to see. Leadership and culture then become a self-reinforcing cycle that can be used as a positive source of competitive advantage or a toxic cycle of failed initiatives, disengagement, and poor results.

CULTURE CHANGE

The exciting news is that with conscious and intentional leadership effort, culture can be managed, changed, and improved. From a baseline perspective, three initial steps begin to help put form and definition around the once nebulous and intangible concept.

First, leaders need to become fully aware of how their culture works. There are many frameworks and culture assessments available to assist leadership in this first step. Additionally, becoming exceptionally observant to how things happen around you begins to shed light on important cultural norms and values.

Second, begin to collect your ideas and desires for your aspirational culture. Leaders can often identify one to three characteristics that they would like to be different.

The third step is often overlooked. It is critical that leaders connect their culture to the organization's strategy. Specifically, articulate the desired results you need your culture to foster to achieve organizational success. Culture is a powerful force that can enable exceptional results, but only if nurtured and designed in alignment with desired outcomes. These three steps are foundational in assisting a leader or leadership team in better understanding what culture is and how to begin to shape it for the future.

For those interested in diving deeper into culture change, there are a few important underlying dynamics worth discussing. With any culture-change initiative, it is key to remember that your current culture is not necessarily bad. It simply is a culture that will not allow you to achieve the results you desire. To achieve new results, we must be clear on the outcomes we desire (as noted earlier) as well as how this shift will require people to think and act differently.

Culture is a persistent way of being for an organization and will not change overnight. To achieve new desired results, you must create shifts in the way people think and act, which then creates new experiences for them to adopt new ways of operating. This sequence creates the conditions for culture change to occur. Getting an organization aligned around culture change does not happen easily. It requires dialogue, engagement, debate, and leadership.

The takeaway is that you have a choice: either you manage your culture, or your culture will manage you. If you look at your organization or team and are not pleased with the results you are getting, take a close look at your culture for ways to improve and begin the work.

HOW AN EFFECTIVE PHYSICIAN LEADER BUILDS CULTURE

With a basic understanding of your culture, leaders can begin to implement strategies to shape the culture going forward. The physician leader is an ideal candidate for leading cultural change work. Physicians are often inherently respected and trusted and typically keep the patient at the forefront of the conversation. However, physicians also need proper skills training and personal development to be set up for success in this work.

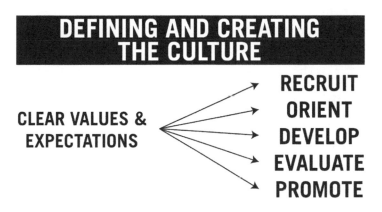

DEFINING AND CREATING THE CULTURE

CLEAR VALUES & EXPECTATIONS

→ RECRUIT
→ ORIENT
→ DEVELOP
→ EVALUATE
→ PROMOTE

Every stage of the employment life cycle needs to be considered with respect to effectively building culture. Again, we must return to the first C of leadership—clarity. Explicit and clearly articulated values and expectations are the critical lifeblood of a strong culture. With clarity, you know exactly what you stand for and where you're going. This cannot be overemphasized as we encounter and lead highly skilled, extremely busy, fiercely independent professionals. If we are not clear in our values, messages, and expectations, we leave them adrift, guessing at what is most important.

The recruitment and selection process is the first point of contact for most potential employees. During this phase, individuals get to know the organization and culture, and leaders get to assess for a sense of cultural fit: does this individual believe what we believe in order to best serve our patients, colleagues, and community?

When I meet a potential future employee during recruitment, I communicate the values and expectations inherent in our culture that we believe in. I begin by being crystal clear. These candidates and new employees hear this during recruitment, the hiring process, and orientation: reinforcement of the clear values and expectations. Then, as part of the professional development, we weave these messages and experiences into the training as well. Leaders who teach this embrace and reinforce the same values and expectations. Then, when they undergo their first evaluation, the same values and expectations are clearly present because they're part of the evaluation process. They see this is what the company stands for. This is what we expect and what we believe in. Then, when people are evaluated and promoted, the whole process has consistency and clarity. The advantage is that you live through it every time you contact, measure, and evaluate people, and it becomes part of the culture. The values and beliefs are woven into the fabric of the organization. The power of clarity and consistency is the impact it has on the newer employee group as they see these values and expectations come to life. It allows them to either: (1) get progressively more bonded and enthused to be part of the organization; or (2) realize there is not a good long-term fit.

Leaders have the responsibility to intentionally create and foster the culture they desire with clarity and consistency in day-to-day actions and behaviors. This, in turn, gives individuals and the organization the opportunity to determine a fit, whether the culture aligns with their own values and beliefs or not.

Here is an example of cultural fit that many physician leaders have likely encountered. I spoke about this for the first time fifteen years ago, during which time people told me that a certain physician was fantastic, and that I needed him on the team. He was described as a gifted surgeon but temperamental, and he threw instruments in the operating room. I was clear that there was no fit for him as that behavior destroys the culture of teamwork, respect, and collaboration, which were core values to the organization. In cases like this, if you don't take a stand with obvious flagrant misbehavior, your credibility is gone, and your culture becomes misaligned. That's why clarity is the number one leadership quality essential to building a strong and healthy culture.

You can likely see how the second C of leadership—consistency—is also critically important to building culture. Having clarity—knowing what you stand for and what is expected—is ground zero. However, without consistency in behaviors and actions, these words quickly lose their meaning. It is critical that leaders behave in ways that support and reinforce the articulated way of being, ways that are absolutely aligned with your values and expectations. Leadership respect and credibility hang in the balance. Leaders find themselves in difficult and professionally damaging situations when they say, "This is what we stand for. This is what we believe in," but when the door closes behind them, their actions do not adhere to their words.

> **⚡ VOLTAGE DROP**
>
> The long-term success, credibility, and trust of this very personal process is dependent on clear values, expectations, and a pristine process of use. When the process is violated by leadership and does not honor the pristine process due to urgency, the message is destructive. It says, "Even though we have taken great pains to develop a fair and open process, sometimes leadership has to take over." This is a true culture killer.

You can talk all you want about building great cultures and teams, but it's worthless if your words and actions don't align, if you blame others for your mistakes, or if you take credit for others' work. Unfortunately, this is quite common and is a telltale sign of a leader who will struggle to build a high-performing culture, team, or organization. Clarity and consistency are paramount to a leader's ability to build a strong and healthy culture.

CRITICAL NEED FOR PHYSICIAN LEADERSHIP TRAINING

In health care, physician leaders don't always begin with deep leadership or management expertise. In my experience, physician leaders often move into leadership roles with little to no actual formal training and development in these areas, and yet we expect physicians to hit the ground running and gracefully lead new teams and manage complex business issues. This dynamic highlights the absolute critical need for physician leadership training. Throughout my entire leadership career, I've dedicated tremendous time and resources to this work to ensure physician leaders felt supported and had the training and skills needed to lead effectively. However, this is by far not the case everywhere and is an incredibly needed and invaluable investment.

Ironically, some believe that the MBA degree will solidify physicians as leaders and that we will finally save health care by giving all doctors MBAs. However, the MBA is like the MD. It's another academic training in acquiring knowledge in a different skillset—business instead of medicine. Neither of these academic degrees confers a comprehensive skillset in leadership, which must also be developed.

From *The Doctor Crisis*:

> Leadership may appear logical and straightforward: focus intensively on the right priorities, and things will click into place. But I found that leadership had all the unpredictability and complexity of a Rubik's Cube in the hands of a novice. To me, connecting dots was a logical and rational exercise, but it was quite different from managing the daily reality of highly complex and highly skilled independent human beings. My central lesson about leadership that emerged over time was that the challenge of leading competent, individual souls is not about logic or compulsion. It's about listening, respect, relentless adherence to values, and sticking to that approach every day—an approach that goes a long way toward repairing a wounded culture.[3]

Another common issue I've seen around physician leadership training is the declaration that it is important, but again, no action occurs to support the claim. Many leaders say the right thing and talk about the importance of physician leadership at a lofty level but fail in execution. To be effective in building great cultures and leaders, executives need to dedicate time and resources for individuals to deeply learn how to be leaders, with

3   Jack Cochran and Charles C. Kenney, *The Doctor Crisis*, 102.

new knowledge, skills, and practices, and how that, in turn, translates into building strong cultures.

I titled this section "Critical Need for Physician *Leadership* Training" with great purpose. Leadership and management often get pooled together as the same concept, but there are important distinctions. The book *Hope Is Not a Method*, written by army generals Gordon R. Sullivan and Michael V. Harper, is about the rebooting of the army after the Vietnam War. In it, the authors explain that management has to do with an organization's processes, and leadership has to do with an organization's purpose. Leadership and management require different skillsets that are not always found in the same individual. A leader may have the skills needed to manage, but a manager may not always have the skills needed to lead.

Similarly, in the words of both Peter Drucker and Warren Bennis, "Management is doing things right; leadership is doing the right things. Management is efficiency in climbing the ladder of success; leadership determines whether the ladder is leaning against the right wall." There is a difference between the two roles, but there is not a bright line between them. In today's world, we need physician leaders who can motivate through purpose and passion, face difficult conversations and decisions, and take the high road. We need physician leaders who can see the forest for the trees and lead health care out of its current challenges.

Building strong culture relies on our ability to have clear values and expectations as well as investing in the professional and personal development of physicians to take on new leadership roles. As stated earlier, leadership and culture are two sides of the same coin. Addressing one side and not the other is a futile effort in change. To gain momentum and success, we need to focus our time, resources, and energy on both critical ingredients!

CASE STUDY ON CULTURE: PERFORMANCE MANAGEMENT AND FEEDBACK

As a leader of large organizations, I have had my share of leadership lessons on how to successfully change culture. These lessons haven't always come easily, and I have had to learn the hard way on occasion. However, I'd like to share a few scenarios that are especially poignant, given the work of physician leaders in today's world of health care.

Never take for granted what performance management, which we discussed in the last chapter, could do to your culture. Here is an example of how small, albeit difficult, changes can make a huge difference.

One of our departments had two problems: the first

problem was a physician with clinical quality issues, and the second problem was a department leader who wasn't managing the first problem. After an evaluation, intervention, and performance improvement plan, we determined the only solution was replacing both individuals. Clearly, leadership was playing a critical role in the toxic culture and outcomes within the team. By making these two changes, conditions vastly improved. We replicated the survey two years later, and satisfaction spiked to more than 80 percent. People don't like working with doctors who hurt patients or staff, or leaders who fail to lead. This one example again highlights the imperative need to have clarity and consistency in building a strong culture.

Be very clear, honest, and consistent in expressing your expectations. If you have a physician who throws instruments, and you do not expunge them, you send a message to your staff that you allow this behavior. It's a litmus test: you promote what you permit. Some of the biggest changes we made at Colorado Permanente Medical Group revolved around how physicians treated their staff, which we incorporated into our evaluation. Following is a perfect example of how dealing with performance issues can drastically improve a team culture and performance.

We had a physician who thought the staff's sole purpose was to make her efficient and help her through their day.

The doctor didn't particularly want to have relationships with any of the team. She told them what she wanted, how she wanted it to work, and if it didn't work, she would be unhappy. The staff turnover was astounding. People rotated out left and right and moved to other places. Finally, the vice president of human resources spoke to the staff. One staff member explained that if we would send the physician to another clinic, the staff would be able to see the same number of patients with just one doctor. Talk about discretionary effort!

When the VP of HR went to this doctor and told her she was being put on a performance improvement plan, it was like lancing a boil. All her venom burst, and she went on a soliloquy about what a bunch of losers these people were, we were, the organization was, and that this was exactly the information she needed to walk out the door. Now, it's possible that physician will go into another practice, create very clear expectations and values, and say, "You want to work here? It's all about productivity. We're going to practice on roller skates. This is what I stand for. This is what we are going to do." Maybe she can find some people who will enjoy that.

Given this, we did not replace that physician position for four months because the staff wanted to prove that they could see the same number of patients without that physician (and heal themselves!). We went to visit this team one afternoon, and the remaining doctor looked like she was a slalom skier. She popped out of one room and ducked into the next room, out of that room and into the next room, and the staff followed her around with amazing enthusiasm and energy. I told her it was fantastic that they could see so many patients a day, but it was time to hire another doctor. It was an interesting experiment though, as the staff genuinely wanted to prove they were not just being wimps and could move mountains in the absence of one toxic player.

As you can see, performance management can be a very challenging task when you are working to change and improve organizational culture. As a physician leader, other physicians often thought it was my job to protect doctors. This was an intrinsic belief that I inherited as I moved into leadership and the very belief I was working to change. I said, "Physician leaders should always support, acknowledge, and reward terrific physicians and provide great environments and careers for physicians, but we must only *protect patients*." This belief became a key point that guided my leadership career, and you will hear me repeat it in this book because it's so critically important yet not intuitive for many of us who, as physicians, have accepted leadership positions.

If a doctor is harming someone else, whether a patient or staff, we don't protect that behavior, and we don't protect that doctor to the exclusion of doing the right thing for the other people. We're reverent and supportive of the profession, but we never allow a title to give people a pass on basic decency and civility toward their fellow man. Expressing a new belief, modeling new behavior, and reinforcing new performance expectations is crucial to shifting a culture, which not only affects productivity, but also the overall well-being of the team and organization.

Feedback and honest performance conversations are cornerstone to the performance management process and become essential for learning and change. When we engage in performance evaluations and find a deficiency or opportunity to improve, we owe it to our colleagues to give the feedback and discuss the performance issue. Recall from chapter 8, if we don't deal with it, the patient suffers, the team suffers, the high performers suffer, and the low performers suffer. The right thing to do is to sit down with people, indicate their strong points and their weak points, and create a performance improvement plan that identifies the areas of deficiency and how we will support the individual to better their situation and the organization as a whole.

Unfortunately, leaders often avoid these difficult conversations and simply let the poor behavior continue.

We will have arrived as a culture when the courageous conversation is considered a thoughtful, humane gift, and when we seek to receive and seek to give critical, constructive feedback.

Only by giving this gift can we support another on a path of change. It is often not easy to do, but the consequence of withholding or ignoring the situation creates suffering on all levels. Leaders who build strong teams, cultures, and organizations find the courage and kindness to provide ongoing feedback and seek it out for themselves as well.

FEEDBACK

Recognition in the form of feedback doesn't always have to be formalized, but to be optimally effective, it should be specific, timely, and directly linked to the values in the work.

If you have a highly valued employee you rely on, who is a high performer and a team player, acknowledge them and be thoughtful in your comments. If you say, "Hey, Sally, you did a fantastic job. We love having you around here. You're an important part of the team," then Sally has no idea what you're talking about. She doesn't know why she's being commended.

Compare those comments with, "Sally, I heard from your colleagues that you came back into the hospital last night because you realized there were three people waiting in the Cath Lab and they were down to one doc and one nursing team. You came back in to do the hardest one, so the other doctors could complete two quickly. The whole team was amazingly enthused by their work that evening, knowing they didn't have a sick patient sitting on hold in preroom for two hours. It made such a difference to everyone, and they were all talking about it." This specific and timely feedback, which is tied to the organization's vision, values, and expectations, is much more impactful than feedback that is not.

One is vague, and the other is timely, specific, linked to the work and the values of the team, and sincere.

Professor Adam Grant at the Wharton School of Business was committed to being a more impactful teacher. His colleague, Sue Ashford, showed him evidence that gathering and acting on negative feedback is how you reach your potential because it signals you are serious about improving. Professor Grant took the student feedback and publicly shared it and committed to his improvement from the very specific criticisms and suggestions. The powerful message to students was that he was listening and that their views were important. They were taken seriously as he and they shaped the course going forward. He has become a consistently top-rated professor at Wharton.[4]

Sheryl Sandberg at Facebook formally institutionalized the importance of the hard conversation by requiring each employee to commit to at least one hard conversation a month, and to increase acceptance, each conversation should go both ways to enrich the outcome. Sheryl encourages beginning these conversations with the sentence, "I'm giving you these comments because I have very high expectations and I know you can reach them."[5]

REWARDS AND RECOGNITION

There is a belief that this profession consists of independent, confident, self-actualized, successful people accustomed to good results and great work and that we don't necessarily absorb energy from people who compliment us. In this book, I have gone into detail about dealing with performance problems and the challenge

---

4   Sandberg and Grant, *Option B*, 149.

5   Sandberg and Grant, *Option B*, 152.

for leaders in dealing with their colleagues who need to change and improve. Despite the honorable goal of this work, it still feels tough and has a toll. Despite the belief that we don't need positive reinforcement, reward and recognition are important to a culture. Reward and recognition are as necessary in the medical field as they are in our daily lives.

The facts around the optimal ratio of positive to negative feedback vary depending on the research. A recent *Harvard Business Review* article states that the average ratio for the highest-performing teams was 5.6 to 1, that is, nearly six positive comments for every negative one. The medium-performance teams averaged 1.9 to 1, almost twice as many positive comments than negative ones. But the average for the low-performing teams, at 0.36 to 1, was almost three negative comments for every positive one.[6]

Even the highly skilled and the capable are very positively influenced by positive feedback, as long as it is specific, timely, and directly linked to the value of their work. It can't be frivolous. People in our profession often downplay its importance, claiming, "We're all professionals. We don't need that rah-rah stuff. We get all

---

6   Jack Zenger and Joseph Folkman, "The Ideal Praise-to-Criticism Ratio," *Harvard Business Review*, March 15, 2013, accessed September 13, 2017, https://hbr.org/2013/03/the-ideal-praise-to-criticism.

our self-actualization from our personal capability and competence." The fact is, this isn't true. We get a lot of secondary gain from acknowledgment. People love to be complimented. Most of us care and recognizing this is vital.

If you institute performance management and have the hard conversations around deficiency, you need to have a ratio of about ten to one positive to negative, and that can be in the form of rewards and recognition. We used to do emails, note cards, and shout-outs at meetings. If you make it goofy and silly, then the professional in all of us brushes it off. But if you stand in front of three hundred doctors and specifically call out someone who performed well, we notice it. We celebrate it.

I realize many of the topics and examples of change mentioned in this chapter may seem difficult at first glance, as they are likely contrary to many of the unspoken beliefs and unwritten rules about how we do things. However, that is the role of a leader when working to change, strengthen, and improve a culture. We need to make explicit the beliefs that are important to moving the culture and be exceptionally consistent in demonstrating the new behaviors needed going forward. This is not easy work, but it is the work that matters to our organizations, to our colleagues, and to our patients.

CHAPTER 11

MENTORS

❓ WICKED QUESTION

Can we only learn from individuals who have more experience or knowledge than we do?

Mentoring provides additional information or knowledge to individuals engaged in the process. It gives them a chance to receive some candid feedback on someone else's perspective of where they're at, where their blind spots are, and where they can leverage some key talents. Mentors also offer resources and connections within and outside organizations for more growth and development. They often offer encouragement and act as a sounding board. Notably, a good mentor breaks people out of their comfort zone. They don't simply tell mentees what they want to hear; they offer a distinct color of reality, essentially giving them mirrors to examine their behaviors and actions in order to improve. We are continuously subjected to inputs and stimuli, just as we're continuously subjected to other people, their behaviors, and how they treat us. Therefore, the importance of mentors is quite substantial.

The power of intellectual humility is not to try to be a more humble, better, or more sensitive person. You simply are profoundly aware that you are surrounded by people who have knowledge and solutions that you don't have. This attitude optimizes your openness to learn and exchange knowledge without a sense that your worth and capability are always being challenged. So much valuable information surrounds you if you have a bit of awareness and openness.

THE TRADITIONAL MENTORING MODEL

The formal traditional mentoring model is the protégé model, with a mentor and mentee who develop a relationship over time. It shouldn't be paternalistic, but it should have a back-and-forth relationship to foster an understanding of one another's points of view and to provide expertise, nuance, or insight. This concept of mutuality is not just about respect, but to ensure the mentor is continually hearing authentic, fresh reactions, feedback, and updates. Anyone who mentors well understands just how much is gained by both parties as they evolve their joint learning journey.

If, as a mentor, you continue to work with an individual and you understand their context, you can also learn from them to improve your work, as well as become a better mentor and teacher. It should be a two-way relationship, with a slight bias toward the more experienced person helping the mentee progress through their learning, but both parties should be learning.

One-on-one mentoring focuses on individual issues beyond simple context sharing and learning additional information. The mentor can also focus on body language and nonverbals. This is important, because if you're lecturing, you don't really get the sense of what the person is thinking. When you have a trusted relationship, you see the brow furrow or the eyes wince and can weigh in at the time. This model has a little less structure and a little more listening, observing, and challenging.

There's an art to it, and the art is simply the openness to acknowledge that you're both there to honor each other's time and different levels of expertise. However, if the mentor doesn't understand how much they can still discover, then the learning process doesn't flourish as much as it can.

The traditional mentoring model often involves people with differences such as education, age, and especially, level of experience. This is usually done in pairs, so you can create enough structure around the topic—like the difficult group—or values and vision of the organization. You promote an atmosphere that allows people to think, talk, and work together. It's necessary to enforce the differences of age, gender, and diversity because we tend to work in packs with people most like us and within our level of an organization.

In official mentoring, people usually meet for about an hour once a month over time, and that duration should be highly individualized based on the needs of the two parties. Some stay on, some switch, but they always decide at the end of an agreed upon time as to whether they'll continue or not. You're not stuck in it, and the value is determined by the two parties. Sometimes a robust relationship may wind down when the parties reach a certain point, but that relationship may also ramp up again in the future as needed. When we had these mentorships, halfway through the year, we brought all the mentors and mentees together through either a lectureship, a book club, or to check in on the current prioritized challenges of the business. While there is some content in these informal gatherings, they're rich in natural conversations about what's occurring within the organization itself. You have the space to ask why and move toward understanding.

THE TRADITIONAL METHOD EVOLVES: COMENTORING

Two members of our team, Drs. Patty Fahy and Andy Lum, introduced another evolution of the traditional mentoring model, comentoring, to our physician group. They loved standard mentoring but thought they would try group mentoring, in which two senior mentors and three or four junior people worked together so that everyone had more ways to observe and learn.

Comentoring gives the group an opportunity to participate in diverse ways beyond the more traditional model so more people can weigh in. Team leaders can become very isolated and out of touch with what happens around them, so having three or four junior people at various levels is important in this mentoring model so they can hear points of view from distinct levels in the organization, which they would never obtain through the traditional model or their own reading or learning journey. The comentoring group discussed topics during long lunches for about ninety minutes a session. The topic could be performance improvement, IT and informatics, health policy, or a variety of topics. One of the senior people might be an on-point leader of the discussion and hand out an article for all to read and discuss. It kept all of them thinking and learning together and was a great gift to the senior leaders to be able to hear impressions from people in different layers of the organization and from different specialties, clinics, and career positions.

These mentoring groups were fascinating. They met once a month for a year before eventually switching to create other groups to continue mixing the diversity of learning. Some of them stayed together unofficially because they enjoyed one another's company and continued to learn and build relationships. As we have pointed out, the implications of complexity in health care have necessitated a new way of providing care and finding solutions including more team-based care and higher levels of collaboration. It is impossible to have too many trusted connections and supportive colleagues. These were all voluntary, and you could always find someone willing to participate. The juniors seemed to like it a lot and perhaps even more than their experiences with one-on-one mentoring. We did at least two of these for two years, so they had two separate groups with different senior and junior leaders. Juniors could then learn enough to become senior mentors themselves someday.

⚡ VOLTAGE DROP

Because of the nature of the group, mentoring groups must be self-governing to ensure the culture is open, fair, and mutually respectful. If a member of a mentoring dyad or a comentoring group misuses the platform or hijacks the agenda, it's the group's responsibility to manage that behavior. The success of the group will require honest intervention and conversation to "true up" the function of the group.

All mentoring is comentoring in a way. The wonderful thing about watching group mentoring is seeing people think on their feet and respond in real time. You can sit quietly and observe people react emotionally and intellectually without the expectation inherent in paired mentoring, where each person must respond to each subsequent input. You not only absorb the content of the topic, but you also learn how people function, how they learn, and how they process demanding situations.

In examining the results experienced by both the mentoring group and the organization, studies find that organizations that make these investments find a decrease in turnover and a promotion of growth. Wharton had a couple of interesting studies, one of which specifically discussed an issue that a lot of physicians face: burnout. They found that someone with an articulated or dedicated mentor experiences less stress and burnout in their jobs. Additionally, they're promoted more rapidly, they're better socialized into the organization, and overall more productive. In response to the question, "How do we help physicians connect to their own purpose and not get completely burned out?" mentoring could be a key ingredient.

The other piece in that same study is related to psychological safety. One of the important ingredients for a mentor-mentee relationship to work is to have a place where one receives psychological and social support—where people can let their guard down and be vulnerable enough to ask tough questions. Without that, you establish more of a transaction of knowledge, not real, meaningful interactions where someone can drop in a little bit more deeply on that more human level.[1]

Lastly, Cleveland Clinic performed an intriguing study that examined the influence of mentoring and role modeling on developing physician leaders. The component that popped out as most beneficial for physician leaders was watching leaders in action. Whether through role modeling, watching someone on a day-to-day basis to gauge the leader's behaviors, or a mentorship engagement, being able to watch a leader in action proved to be one of those critical components.

Many of the respondents in this study favored a series of strategic interactions with various individuals about specific professional issues rather than the traditional long-term longitudinal mentoring experience. We've seen folks go to different people for different issues. That's a healthy and advantageous way to look at more of the topical areas for mentorship and content development.

1   "Workplace Loyalties Change, but the Value of Mentoring Doesn't," *Knowledge@Wharton*, March 16, 2007, accessed September 13, 2017, http://knowledge.wharton.upenn.edu/article/workplace-loyalties-change-but-the-value-of-mentoring-doesnt.

There's almost a parallel reality to the discussion about the world consisting of simple problems, complicated problems, and complex problems. If you talk about simple problems such as, "How do you go from here to there?" a mentor can be immensely capable in terms of short answers. "This is how you do it. This is why this is the right answer." Complicated problems require some journey, sharing, and teaching, but moving into complexity doesn't lend itself to the model of the gradient of expert and student. It doesn't work for those quick, pithy answers, but it also means that both student and teacher must be engaged in a growth experience because complexity doesn't allow anybody to have that much power.

People in mentor relationships can tackle simple and complicated problems within the traditional boundaries of their relationship and get to solutions together with enough time and effort. This world of increasing complexity challenges us anew to learn how to learn! In other words, the learning may be better focused on approaches and processes to deal with complex issues, including identifying additional valued colleagues to bring in to the thinking.

You can be very surface-level with simple things and if you need to go deep into those complex issues, it requires both the mentee and mentor to let their guards down and be vulnerable. Accept that no one has the answer so you can dive in and figure it out together.

MENTORS EVERYWHERE

We have defined two important types of mentoring. The first is the traditional, formal model, with a mentor and mentee. The second one is the comentoring model, which involves a flexible, mutable, learning community in which we deploy different people, diverse groups, different topics, and different skillsets for open group learning.

There is a third type of mentoring that is widely accessible yet often overlooked and rarely acknowledged, which I refer to as "mentors everywhere." This third form of mentoring is the day-to-day sharing of knowledge, experience, expertise, and insight provided by people you see every day in a dozen different situations. For this, you need to be mindful. If I can't watch and learn from a colleague who is dealing with a demanding situation—if my mind is preoccupied and fixated on something else—I can't learn.

Seventy-nine percent of millennials see mentoring as a crucial aspect of their career success,[2] but they're likely connecting with mentors in a nontraditional manner. They could be looking at peers as mentors or individuals in other departments or in different industries and sectors. That refines the definition of mentor. Traditionally,

---

2   Julie Kantor, "Four Key Benefits of Workplace Mentoring Initiatives," *The Blog* (blog), *Huffington Post*, March 11, 2016, accessed September 13, 2017, http://www.huffingtonpost.com/julie-kantor/four-key-benefits-of-work_b_9432716.html.

a mentor relationship might have implied some sort of gradient for superiority of knowledge and experience, whereas this new form of mentoring focuses on awareness and mindfulness. If you can't learn through everyday interactions, you miss out. Look at different people and how they behave. The world is a rich place from which to learn. You just have to be aware, open, and discerning with a nice dose of humility, which grounds you as one who can learn from many sources.

Mentoring gained through awareness and mindfulness is available throughout your daily journey. We should always seek wisdom from people. I often find, when talking to people who externally appear to have very challenging socioeconomic realities but who are cheerful, articulate, thoughtful, and interesting, their woes have no traction to keep their spirits down. There's so much to gain there. Then I watch other people, with everything going for them, who just drag through life.

Mentors and mentees everywhere share their knowledge and learn from mindfulness and presence. We need to be mindful and to notice. We need to have a sense of what's going on and be able to question why people are so positive when they don't have the title or education people assume comes with happiness. Ask yourself why you find a situation interesting, concerning, or confusing, and what you can learn from it.

Notice, listen, and be able to pause and learn without being completely preoccupied. There are mentors everywhere who can provide you with indelible lessons on how you do or don't want to be. It's not that this occurs every minute of every day, but you miss out if you don't watch people and remain curious.

> ### 🔑 KEY POINT
>
> Endless learning opportunities exist when we observe people and understand the impact of their behavior and their words.

While watching a grocery-store employee bag groceries, I turned to my grandson and said, "Isn't that interesting?" This man was about seventy-five years old and he was having a ball, and people really related to him. I said to my grandson, "I don't know anything about that man, but he is creating an aura around him of real positivity." He was doing more to improve productivity than the manager was.

He was just a stitch. His entire workspace was probably ten feet by fifteen feet. He wasn't being crass or stupid. He was just on a roll, entertaining us with his energy and banter about groceries. He was wearing a little headband and good grocery-issue shorts, and the grocery bags were his instruments. He chose to make the day a wonderful day—all at nine o'clock in the morning. Many of us had a better day because of this person. There could be lots of layers to that story, and I don't know the salary of someone who bags groceries, but I bet it's less than fifteen dollars an hour. These are the kinds of moments that give me energy and a nice chance to self-reflect on how I impact my ten-by-fifteen-foot space in life.

I used to gauge the new hires on my teams by what they did to my personal level of energy. After working with people for a while, sometimes I realized they were sucking the energy out of my soul. I had to recognize that and do something about it if I could. Energy is a great gift. You can get a lot of it from people around you if you have the right people in the right environments and the right access.

I once visited a game park in Africa after a surgery trip, where we completed six days of major reconstructive surgical procedures at an urban hospital. One of the nurses who worked with us in the operating room lived in a hut in a rural village. She took a local bus to the hospital, and at the end of the week, she took the same bus back to her village in the bush. These buses were packed well beyond the capacity of the seats. She spent every weekend in her village, where she took care of her family, the goats, the chickens, and more. On the Friday after we finished our week of surgery, we headed out for a weekend in a game park as tourists. On the way, we saw her waiting in line to get on the bus, and the driver was speaking to her. We were about to go to the game park for a photo safari when our driver asked us if this nurse could sit in the front seat of our Land Rover with him. Her village was near the game park, so we said of course she could come. It would save her money and the experience of sitting on a sixty-seat bus with one hundred people.

We were just transitioning from the city to the agricultural part of the environment—where you see goats, lambs, and cattle—to the wilderness. Suddenly, she and the driver started talking rapidly. The driver pulled over and pointed out a couple of cheetahs.

The three of us—an anesthesiologist and two surgeons—were in the back armed with Nikons, Pentaxes, and all these dueling photographic machines. We took countless pictures, and the nurse asked the driver for some binoculars. He extracted a crusty old pair of binoculars some tourist had probably left twenty years ago.

As they looked, the nurse said, "What do you think about that scar on that older cheetah's nose?"

The driver said, "I was looking at that. I think that's from a lion, don't you?"

She responded, "I do too. That's a lucky cheetah, if that's all the lion got."

Through the laughter, she looked back at the three of us changing lenses, filters, and jabbering away, and said, "What do you see?"

One of us said, "Oh, we have several great photos of these two cheetahs."

Another one of us asked, "Why do you ask?"

She looked up at us, and the only description for the look on her face was empathy. She said, "I think you guys have so much that it keeps you confused."

Her reaction was to feel sorry for us because we looked confused. We discussed it that night over an African lager, wondering what it was all about, when my colleague said, "It was obvious that she and Moody, the driver, were one with the cheetahs. They were with the cheetahs, and we were documenting the cheetahs." Our interaction with the cheetah had an underlying purpose to make a three-by-four-foot blowup on the wall of our den, and theirs was to be with the cheetah. I thought that was amazing. That was the lesson from the nurse, an everyday mentor.

In a similar vein, in 1984, I once went on another surgical mission trip to Manila, Philippines, with an anesthesiologist and four US plastic surgeons for ten days of teaching and performing reconstructive surgery. We were all technically close to our prime and doing pretty good work in our daily practices back home. In Manila, we had interesting cases and worked with a group of bright, eager Filipino general surgery residents who were there to help us and learn.

We weren't arrogant and presumptuous, but we were caught off guard by one of the residents.

Dr. Victor Poronshuckula was a second-year surgery resident at the hospital. The first day, one of us used his assistance, and later that night, the doctor told us Victor was one of the most gifted kids he had ever worked with. The next day, another one of us worked with Victor, and that night, we all went out to dinner and talked about this resident.

The doctor who had worked with him that day said, "I paid attention because this is a second-year general surgery resident that you are all finding exceptional, which is pretty unusual because you're used to working with seventh-year plastic surgery residents."

By the third day, we were stunned. We had yet to define and understand what we were observing.

After working with Victor, I realized that when I asked him questions, he responded with the knowledge the others had communicated to him. He was not only a quick learner but also grasped the nuances of the patient's deformity and the distortion of the normal anatomy.

For instance, I asked him, "Victor, what do you think about this lip?"

He said, "Well, Dr. Cochran, I think this looks like the one Dr. Hague told me was best treated this way because of these features. But I don't know. What do you think?"

I thought he made a good point for an inexperienced young man. What he gained in three days had depth I found incomprehensible.

We drew the blue line indicating where we would cut, and he interjected, "I worry about this. Dr. Hague said this part of the nose is so short that it's hard to get it to look normal."

He was right.

He continued, "Would it help if we use that little C-flap that you taught me?"

It would, so I allowed him to do the whole surgery while I observed, making comments. I wasn't irrelevant—that's my story and I'm sticking to it. But I did watch him, his demeanor, how he handled the tissue, and the way the staff related to him.

Victor was accomplishing tasks as well as or better than I did after fifteen years as a fully trained plastic surgeon. Yes, he had the gift of skillful hands, but he also had a respectful and positive approach and an almost serene demeanor in the operating room. It was as if the operating room slowed down when he entered.

On the fourth night, I had a proposal. I told my colleagues we needed to spend the next four days learning as much from Victor as we could. They all laughed. I insisted that this kid had a sense of reverence for the difficulty and complexity of the situation and the patient that made him focused, mindful, and attentive. There was a temple-like quality in the operating room when Victor was there because people took their cues from him. He was a quiet, respectful man. He was so technically gifted, it was scary. He was very fortunate for his God-given talent, but his aura also came from his demeanor of professionalism and respect that came across as reverence.

He never said a word of advice to us. He simply repeatedly thanked us. It wasn't gratuitous, but it shocked us. I left the Philippines saying, "I have to be more like Victor. I have to be more mindful, more aware, and more respectful in my approach to my own work."

I had another great life lesson like this in East Africa. This time, my son Ryan was with me. Unfortunately, as is the case around the globe, women supported their society. They did the heavy lifting and the arduous work. They were the glue, the spirituality of the community, of the family, and of the village, and they got all the dirty work. The men went out and hunted or herded and did a lot of hanging out. Women supported the villages, families, and children.

In the rainy season, the women got their five-liter clay pots, put them on their heads, and went to the local mud holes to obtain water to take back to their hut to boil for cooking and cleaning. But in the dry season, all the mud holes were dry, and they would have to walk several kilometers to get any water. They put these clay pots on top of their heads and went along a trail holding hands, singing, and laughing with one another, and sometimes even found safe spaces away from lions if they had to stay the night. I remember thinking fourteen hours was a long day in the dry season. When they returned to their village, they boiled the water and cooked with it.

As Ryan and I watched, my son said to me, "Look at those women, Dad. They're so happy."

I asked him if he could imagine me saying to him, "Ryan, I'd like you to walk fourteen hours today to get me five liters of water so I can have dinner tonight."

He said, "Yeah, I don't think you would ask me that."

I said, "No. Nobody is asking them to do it either. So what are the things that you see that they have that we should know about?"

He told me he believed they found happiness where they were, so they must appreciate something around them.

"And," he added, "patience. The world has to slow down enough to make it worth it to spend fourteen hours getting a few liters of water."

They had toughness and tenacity, but this wasn't a notable event for them. We were watching their daily lives. Their attitude and demeanor made all the difference. The traits we observed by watching them were appreciation, joy, patience, and tenacity. The next time you're hiking and run out of water or have a problem with your buckle on your ski boot and want to spend the next hour pissing and moaning, remember these women. There's something to be learned here.

My last example of these monumental insights gets to the core of an American and global dilemma today. During the challenging political reality of 1981, I was among a team of surgeons on a humanitarian quest in a small town in Nicaragua. We worked alongside a Nicaraguan nurse anesthetist, and a Guatemalan general practitioner who was trying to move to the United States but struggling with the medical license exams. He helped us on the wards and with recovering post-op patients.

The GP also played baseball there. At lunch, we pitched baseballs, which he would send a thousand miles, it seemed. One time, he hit one into the jungle, and I went to fetch it. I saw this giant structure—which I thought was a building—but it was a jet. I ran to get my camera, and then sprinted back into the jungle to take a few pictures.

After a few clicks of my camera, I suddenly heard other *click, click, clicks.* Guns! I was surrounded by ten young men, and they were all carrying AK-47s. The jet I was photographing was a Russian MiG, and these young soldiers were part of the Nicaraguan Sandinista army.

They marched me, a blue-eyed gringo, back to the baseball field, where my boss cursed and yelled, "What did you do?"

I said, "Well, I took a picture."

He swore and asked, "What of?"

"A MiG," I said.

He swore again, then added, "The only question here is

what's going to happen to me, because as far as you are concerned, if they don't kill you, I will."

We were put in the back of a Jeep and taken to Puerta Cabezas, where we were arrested and interrogated for two and a half hours.

Our Spanish-speaking interrogators didn't have any immigration records on us and couldn't figure out who we were. They didn't have phones, but they did have a telegraph. Finally, their Chinese commandant came in and with a perfect English accent, yelled and berated us. They sent us back to Managua, and our surgical tour of the Mosquito Coast ended.

The US ambassador in Managua woke us up at 5:00 a.m. and told us to meet him in the hotel lobby. Relations were very tense, he said, and what in the hell did we think we were doing? He left no doubt of how stupid and risky our (my) actions had been.

Our reservations to fly back to the United States were a week out. In the meantime, we were put to work in a government hospital with a plastic surgeon, an anesthesiologist, and a couple of other surgeons. These guys didn't want us there, but they were stuck with us.

The chairman of the department—my boss, as I was the

chief resident back at home—told me we would be operating with the local surgeon, Dr. Fidel. He said, "We've got to do these cases, and they have to go well. We need to ensure it looks like he's doing it because he doesn't have great training."

Dr. Fidel was in his forties, the chairman was in his sixties, and I was in my thirties, so the chairman proposed we act like he's the professor and rave about how good Dr. Fidel is to make it through the week. Many of the cases were very challenging and complicated, and most of them had already been operated on a time or two. During that week, the other doctors realized we had good surgical skills. They somewhat warmed up to us and even went out to dinner with us on Thursday night, though it was brief and not overly friendly.

The last day, before we caught our plane, they took us out on Lake Nicaragua. Interestingly, the lake was home to sharks. We tooled around on this little rented launch that was so porous the owner's sons were bailing water the whole time. The anesthesiologist—who had been in Nicaragua his whole life, other than two years of college in Miami—brought out a bottle of Flor de Caña rum and proposed a toast.

This man, who we had seen in scrubs all week, now donned a pair of shorts, revealing a giant scar running up his leg. It was a gunshot wound, we learned, a memento from his time as a soldier fighting the Somocistas when the Sandinistas came into power.

"This scar represents everything I hate about you guys," he said, then continued. "I was born to hate gringos, and I have always hated gringos." He held up the bottle of rum, and toasted, "But you guys are OK. We had a great week."

We had been thrown into a situation where it was impossible to tell who was the communist and who was the capitalist, taken care of Nicaraguan citizens, and operated in a very democratic manner. It was, for me, illuminating.

What is the depth of hatred? What is the depth of bias? What is the depth of "I hate you, but if I get to know you more, I have a harder time hating you?" Sometimes you dislike people more when you get to know them, but sometimes not.

Pay attention. There are mentors all around us.

CONCLUSION

APPLYING HEALER, LEADER, PARTNER

> **❓ WICKED QUESTION**
>
> Where will physicians be when health care is transformed?

In the past several decades, the day-to-day reality of patients hasn't changed that much. They still have issues with just not feeling well and being sick. But, for physicians, much has changed for us, around us, and in knowledge and technology.

Dealing with ever-increasing complexity and change is an issue that continually challenges physicians. From the physician's point of view, we have not fully embraced or led these changes that have been cumulative and significant over time. We have had commitment to maintaining a high level of medical clinical knowledge. We read our journals and attend educational meetings, but that has become overwhelmingly complex because of the number of studies and journals.

The commitment to continual learning and growth must include understanding technology, embracing the unusual ways we acquire and see knowledge, and analyzing how our data, analytics, machine learning, and artificial intelligence impact the world we work in. The other option is being left behind by a lot of bright people trying to solve problems around us or without us. To embrace a platform of improvement means we must continue to be curious, committed to learning, and pursue this with the intention of personal growth.

Continual learning requires more than keeping up with your medical literature. Challenge yourself with learning and developing other skills, such as informatics or IT. Continually refresh the work and the group that you work with. It's important to be a personal learner, and to model that growth by challenging your team to embrace this change.

INTENTIONALITY OF LEARNING

Learning should not be one of the stops along the way. You're not just checking a box. Have quarterly lectures. Bring in innovative speakers from both your own and other disciplines, such as people with advanced thinking that are not from your field.

People may ask, "Where'd you find this guy? What is he doing?"

"Well, this is what he's doing," you tell them. "He's trying to lead the first rocket ship to Mars."

"What does that have to do with health care?"

"Well, what he's doing is almost impossible, and there has to be some sense of courage, relentlessness, et cetera, to get there."

You must give people's circuitry a little buzz or a tweak, or they get stuck. They get mired in thinking, "This is where we are, and this is where we're going," but we're not getting there very quickly.

Intentional learning isn't just about reading terrific books. It's about reading great books, having great conversations, and modeling what you seek to embody. Have book clubs, training programs, leadership exchanges, and lectureships. Have people from one department spend time in other departments. Institute a continuous sense of modeling, learning, and changing. The intentionality indicates that you live leadership.

We did book clubs for a while, but when one person communicated to me that nobody had picked a book for the fourth quarter, I told them to cancel it. When this person objected, I explained that until someone came to me with fire in their message, claiming everyone had to read a certain book, the club would be a waste of time. Instead, we brought a speaker in to talk about mindfulness. As you see, it relates back to the notion of modeling, rather than ticking off boxes.

STAND UP. DON'T SIT ON THE SIDELINES

Another important aspect of intentionality and learning relates to a prominent challenge in leadership, which is being true to your beliefs. We say learning is important, but then we have no time for it. We tell people to go take courses, as opposed to having the CEO at the forefront of the learning experience, perhaps leading book clubs. The nature of intentionality is walking the talk and making these things more pervasive than interventional. Senior leaders must both participate in learning efforts and also lead where suitable.

There is a potential for a learning practice to stagnate. Say, "OK, we have the surgery department lecture every Friday. Do we ever cancel it? Do we ever have somebody come in and talk about yoga?" When you have these expectations and boxes to check, you must be mindful that you don't simply do something to fill a time slot. Be prepared to change things, cancel things, and try new and different things. Sometimes your priorities change. Perhaps a group of surgeons was originally going to discuss lung cancer at a meeting, and you decide to change the subject to hatred and violence in the community, for example. These shifts also allow the group to see themselves and each other through a different lens.

Learning is continuing to find new ways to challenge, stimulate, and learn. Don't be too limited by traditions, time, schedules, or preexisting patterns.

The comentoring model and the signal generator model were homegrown, and neither one of them had a life of ten years. We did them for a while, and other people didn't pick them up or didn't like them. It would be nice if those practices endured because they're valuable, but if they reached the end of their usefulness, that's fine too. When that happens, you must ask about the next way of stimulating groups and individuals to learn faster and together. Maybe the signal generator will return when you need it. You don't have to kill something forever; it can come back when necessary. It's all about being active, not passive.

THE CHALLENGE

🔑 **KEY POINT**

We must fortify the patient's voice in health care through clinician (physician) leadership and accountability.

The issues are clear, and the challenges are great, and it is essential that physician leadership—with full expression of compassion, humanity, and ability to influence—continues its dedication to provide patients and families with a quality experience with health care and a renewed hope for their American dream.

We must become an inspired and mobilized group of idealists and activists who continue to honor and leverage the high ground of healer, to transform health care on behalf of our patients by embracing and strengthening the mantle of leader, and to define and enhance the role of partner. This book provides proven and practical information and guidance for physician leaders at all levels of development. This learning journey should be well grounded in strong basics and prepare you for continuous development and growth as a leader.

By now, I hope I have made the case that physicians should view their accountability and responsibilities much more broadly than we have in the past. At one time, we just had to be good doctors. Today, patients have issues with affordability, access, and other health care challenges and obstacles, so it's up to us to be more broadly involved. This is the physician as leader. It is still very important to be trusted, capable, and compassionate physician healers, but we can provide leadership and influence all these other challenges facing the system and our patients. It is not only what we can do, but what we must do.

Patients are not hoping for a perfect insurance plan or the ideal legislation. All they want is affordable access to safe care. And what they need and deserve is care that is safe, equitable, accessible, affordable, and centered on them. The challenges are considerable, the opportunities for strong leadership are critical, and the work required must result in a clinical care system that meets all these requirements patients need and deserve.

FOUR ESSENTIAL ACTIONS

The breadth of the impact of health care and the magnitude of its impact mean improvements must extend from individual contributions all the way to creating effective systems of care. To create this future of transforming health care, physicians need to accept four essential actions:

1. Opt in and lead with unwavering awareness of the true reality of our patients.
2. Structure for efficacy and excellence.
3. Develop a culture of measurement and improvement.
4. Promote a learning community.

OPT IN AND LEAD WITH UNWAVERING AWARENESS

Physicians need to opt in and lead with an unwavering awareness of the reality of patients and families as they experience the health care system. This deep and clear understanding of this reality of our patients is an essential step as we examine our sense of personal mission and compare our reality today, as ourselves, with the twenty-one-year-old idealist writing an application to medical school.

Though we have shared great advances in improving health and health care for patients during our careers focused as healers, many issues and problems remain as stark realities for our patients and families. We must leverage the deserved, high ground of healer to embrace the roles of leader and partner to solve the issues of safety, equity, equality, access, and affordability.

While we don't like all the changes that have happened to us and around us, the covenant and responsibility to patients is clearer than ever. I challenge us to examine our personal mission by refining and rebooting it to the lens of a leader who is seriously needed by patients and families to step up and lead important change. This commitment must include what we need to improve now, but also a keen view of the next five to ten years so we don't get caught unaware again.

To realize this commitment to be responsible, we must also commit to continuous personal learning and development as a leader and to develop a growing coalition of leaders around us.

STRUCTURE FOR EFFICACY AND EXCELLENCE

Much has been written of the advantages of systems of care, such as Kaiser Permanente, Mayo Clinic, Intermountain Healthcare, Cleveland Clinic, Geisinger, and so on. These systems are held up as structural models that deliver excellent health care, and support for these kinds of organizational systems has appeared through the health policy and health reform legislation and discussion.

The Institute of Medicine (now called the National Academy of Medicine), in its 2001 sentinel publication *Crossing the Quality Chasm* noted that working harder in the current system, or lack of a system, would not solve the unmet problems in health care. The Institute stated that organizations must successfully negotiate six major challenges:

1. Redesigning care processes based on best evidence.
2. Effective use of information technology.
3. Knowledge and skills management.
4. Development of effective teams.
5. Coordination of care across conditions, services, and settings.
6. Use of performance in outcomes for continuous improvement and accountability. Addressing these challenges requires that certain structural and investment priorities be accepted, and physicians must adopt the roles of leader and partner.

Cornerstones of the idealized future system include attention to quality (Medicare Star Bonuses), structure (Accountable Care Organizations, or ACOs), payment innovation (bundled payment and capitation), and affordability (product design and payment levers).

Meaningful responses to these varied issues are extremely limited by small medical practice business, isolated doctors, or hospitals that are not part of a system. While the systems mentioned differ in some ways, they share some common features:

1. They know their true north—their direction and their mission. These systems were founded and designed to attain a specific mission of quality and efficiency of health care delivery. Clarity of the organization's values and destination are established and supported, and all strategic and operational decisions and behaviors are aligned. Simon Sinek might observe that these organizations know their why and live it.

2. Physician group practice. When physicians practice in small isolated practices, they have almost no voice outside the confines of their office to influence insurance companies, hospitals, or the government. When they aggregate around personal interests, such as specialty societies and large clinical mergers, they have a voice, but it's often oriented toward the needs of the physician with a variable voice about the needs of the patient. However, when physicians aggregate around the needs of patients to create and improve a system that prioritizes issues like clinical quality, efficiency, and affordability, there develops a unified voice worthy of an audience.

3. Integration with alignment, which starts by putting

the structural pieces together and then optimizing alignment among the entities. For example, many doctors may be working together at a hospital, but if they are not headed in the same direction, they're structurally integrated but not aligned in focusing their energy and capabilities on a common goal. True alignment requires us to not only work together but also share a mission.

When organizations have their clear sense of why, then the development of physician group practice and true functional integration becomes possible and (per Sinek) to develop the discipline of how to consistently deliver the what of the results you aspired to attain.

Morten Hansen, in his book *Collaboration*, quotes the 9/11 Commission findings of what went wrong on September 11, when so much information was held by so many organizations, including the FBI, CIA, FAA, military, police, and secret service, but they failed to collaborate. When the 9/11 Commission tried to explain what went wrong, they said,

> The decentralized structure was sharply criticized by the 911 Commission, which noted that the agencies are like a set of specialists in a hospital, each ordering tests, looking for symptoms and prescribing medication. What is missing

is the attending physician who makes sure they work as a team.[1]

How dreadful is that for physicians? The 9/11 Commission, at a moment of the lowest morale in the history of our lives, used hospital specialists as an example to explain to the public how bad the situation was. Thankfully, much has changed in health care since those words were written, but there is still much to do. What does integration look like when it is most effective? There is an unwavering focus on the mission and values of the organization expressed via collaboration and partnership with a continuous focus on the needs of the patient. Then the entities or departments within the integrated system collaborate, cooperate, and optimize across departmental or organizational areas to align thinking, behaviors, and decisions on needs of the patient. At its most effective, it is clear and easy to see physicians fulfilling all the roles of healer, leader, and partner.

1. We must invest in leadership and learning for organizations with a clear and unwavering commitment to quality, safety, and improvement. Essential enablers for investment include:
   A. Information technology. Highly functional and user-friendly systems require high software and

---

1   Morten Hansen, *Collaboration: How Leaders Avoid the Traps, Build Common Ground, and Reap Big Results* (Boston: Harvard Business Review, 2009).

hardware standards as well as comprehensive training and support, both financial and with time, to ensure the value is realized by the very busy user. We must also stay current with technological developments and make strategic and thoughtful investments in them because they are central to our clinical view of the world.

B. Leadership training and development. As we have discussed throughout this book, a lack of investment here creates major deficiencies in capability and execution to realize value in leading improvement and change.

C. Leadership time and support. Leadership is not effective when it's only deployed two evenings a month. For physicians to focus on priorities and leadership challenges, they need supported free time from the urgency of their practice.

The inherent bias of all physicians is patient first, and that needs to be understood, respected, and included in the planning for time and space for physicians to have meaningful leadership roles.

2. We must influence externalities. This starts with a clarifying apology. Early in this book, in referencing physicians being victims, I challenged them to stop blaming everyone and everything—the lawyers, the legislatures, the ACA, pharmaceutical compa-

nies, insurance companies, and hospitals—and not revert to the role of victim as the basic tenets of being accountable, responsible physician leaders. Remember that eighty-three cents of every health care dollar is spent due to decisions made by physicians and patients, so much remains to focus on in our delivery of clinical care.

However, many other factors influence quality, cost, access, and equity, and these external forces affect the outcome and the present state. Externalities such as the legal system, pharmaceutical companies, insurance companies, governments, and employers are all influencers. The power of systems of care, as opposed to individuals, is we can create and act in ways that influence many of these stakeholders. Systems can ensure that the right voices are heard.

DEVELOP A CULTURE OF MEASUREMENT AND IMPROVEMENT

Physicians must develop a culture of measurement and improvement with an unwavering awareness of patient needs and impact. When organizations have a clear and desirable sense of mission, direction, and values, and they invest to structure for efficiency and effectiveness, the pieces are in place for improvement.

Developing the organizational oversight and team to

agree on the measures that are most important initiates the development of the culture. The process of measurement and transparency provides a true view of the present state and the platform to track and compare for improvement. When measures align with mission, transparency adds the fuel to find ways to move to improvement. The cycle of measure, acknowledge, compare, learn, and improve can then be self-perpetuating.

A close look at the integrated systems described above reveals how they have built cultures and organizations with the capabilities and the clear sense of direction to continuously focus on improvement and innovation.

PROMOTE A LEARNING COMMUNITY

In chapter 1, my fourth question to leaders was, "How broad is our sense of personal mission?" The dilemma is whether we accept responsibility for our broader community beyond our own subset of the population. Today, most health care organizations are insular with a focus on their own operational and financial performance, and this focus informs how they view and relate to their competitors. While we will always need to be competitive, we are also community citizens and stewards and should explore opportunities to collaborate to improve the health of the entire community.

It sounds impressive for health care to become a learning

industry, but this large aspiration can only be realized by focusing on the performance of accountable units to ensure the learning develops and spreads.

These accountable units are: (1) Coalitions of Organizations; and (2) Communities.

Let's take a closer look at two important areas of these units, clinical learning and community collaboration.

Clinical Learning

The daily operational challenges of any health care organization are many and varied, and each organization has areas of outstanding performance and of deficiency. The power of a learning coalition is collective intelligence and learning, and strong support from colleagues.

Member organizations that convene this kind of robust learning include IHI, ACHP, AMGA, AAMC, AMA, and AHA. They enjoy a rich environment to learn and get answers to hard problems. The community collaboration challenge is being open to sharing clinical advances, including with competitors, for the good of the community.

At Kaiser Permanente, we always focused on clinical quality in our regional business units and had very strong results. But as we got more data and transparently comparable data, we could see significant variation. Leadership took this seriously, and from 2008 to 2015, we had a great journey of individual and collective improvement enabled by a community of sharing and learning. The power of collaboration and community learning was impressive.

Another example of a learning coalition was referenced in chapter 1 in the discussion of Choosing Wisely. This effort started with the sponsorship of the American Board of Internal Medicine and has continued to attract many organizations learning from the original participants and adding their own new learning.

Communities

Any time an organization has major performance improvements through its own internal learning or shared learning from an organizational coalition, a dilemma of competition versus collaboration exists regarding sharing new improvements.

In chapter 1, we referenced the collaboration between hospitals in London to create the best system to care for stroke patients. The best pathway to care for these patients was a consolidation of venues of care to a small number of well-placed, highly competent, well-resourced units. This process epitomized putting the patient first to crcate the best possible solution, while accepting the consequences that certain good hospitals were not part of the network. We need to remember this when we potentially create duplicate services in our communities.

We must continue to be agile in how we learn about and include all this wonderful technology and advancement. We must understand that fear and uncertainty will require a trusted ear, a trusted voice, and a trusted person to work with. As the leader, you can see no technology is integrated, comprehensive, or good enough to solve all the big problems of health care, and we need to be in the center of that from a leadership point of view, not by trying to block the progress or improvement but by continuing to gauge, monitor, advance, and shape it, so it's as good as it can be. That role of leadership should never be taken away from us. No doubt, the emergence and development of IT, big data, analytics, algorithms, artificial intelligence, machine learning, and unforeseen advances will have a major impact—and radically affect the work and reality for physicians—but it will be up to us to learn and grow to ensure that we continue to be that trusted source for connection between these capabilities and our vulnerable patients who require a human touch.

The role of partner dictates that we find new and diverse ways to use ourselves, our teams, and our partners, because the old days of everything running through the doctor's office are gone forever—and should be. We partner not only with nurses, pharmacists, and other physicians, but also with great analytical teams, IT departments, code developers, and other people finding ways to solve problems. The limitation is the interface between complexity and the human brain.

The role of healer is our most grounded and important commitment. We must never lose that focus because there will be very difficult decisions that patients and families have to make, and even though they will get their knowledge, information, and potential decisions from lots of other resources, they will want a trusted person who cares for them, cares about them, listens, and helps them make decisions.

It's our time, it's our turn, and patients need us. Let's stand up and move forward because we may be in transition or unhappy, but the role of patient is not getting easier anytime soon. The world is changing all around us. Not everyone is sympathetic to us and waiting for us to feel better.

My hope is that this book gives you a compilation of learning lessons, skills, and confidence to adapt to these changing times and to deal with the issues that patients and families face beyond the clinical.

Despite advances, miracles, cures, and unprecedented improvement in health care quality and delivery, we still have major problems of uneven quality, inequitable access, and affordability.

As physicians, we have the influential position of knowledge, credibility, and trust, and can help people from a quality of care and intelligent spending point of view. We can help manage the cost of health care with our own decisions, and those of the patient, with our influence in the doctor-patient interaction. By doing so, we can help people reboot their version of the American dream.

The American dream is faltering. We need to restore hope and give some of the 18 percent of GDP currently spent on health care back to the American people. Ultimately, within each of us must be the resolve. Resolve is not about demanding work and dedication. Those are the table stakes. It's a relentless focus on the reality and the mission. The future is going to be tough, but it is in our hands. We have the ability and talent to create that inflection point to transform health care and restore the American dream for future generations. Our patients, families, and communities are depending on us. What kind of ancestor will you be?

To my fellow physicians: thank you for your commitment to...

- Honor and leverage healer
- Embrace and strengthen leader
- Define and enhance partner

Onward!

BOOKS FOR ASPIRING PHYSICIAN HEALERS, LEADERS, AND PARTNERS

When accepting a different role or even a new occupation, the need for education and learning are considerable. There are countless options, including seminars, courses, blogs, and journal articles. While all of these are useful and helpful, an in-depth study of particular subjects is often well-served by excellent books that represent a major body of focused professional effort by the authors.

As part of my venture into leadership, I have benefited from and continue to learn from all these modalities, including reading hundreds of books on related subjects.

From this experience, I challenged myself to select a few that I felt were particularly valuable. This list is very diverse in terms of topic, publication date, writing style, and author's background. This eclectic list does not pretend to be comprehensive nor focused on a central theme, but it does offer a broad view of themes and views impacting leaders. Enjoy, add your own, and let me know what I need to read next!

—JC

Collins, Jim. *Good to Great: Why Some Companies Make the Leap...And Others Don't*. New York: Harper Collins, 2001.

Covey, Stephen R. *The Seven Habits of Highly Effective People*. New York: Fireside, 1989.

Edmondson, Amy C. *Teaming: How Organizations Learn, Innovate, and Compete in the Knowledge Economy*. Boston: Jossey-Bass, 2012.

Goleman, Daniel, Richard Boyatzis, and Annie McKee. *Primal Leadership: Unleashing the Power of Emotional Intelligence*. Boston: Harvard Business Review, 2002.

Hansen, Morten. *Collaboration: How Leaders Avoid the Traps, Build Common Ground, and Reap Big Results*. Boston: Harvard Business Review, 2009.

Hawken, Paul. *The Ecology of Commerce: A Declaration of Sustainability*. New York: Harper Business, 1993.

Kouzes, James M. and Barry Z. Posner. *Encouraging the Heart: A Leader's Guide to Rewarding and Recognizing Others*. San Francisco: Jossey-Bass, 1999.

McKeown, Greg. *Essentialism: The Disciplined Pursuit of Less*. New York: Crown Business, 2014.

Pfeffer, Jeffrey. *Dying for a Paycheck: How Modern Management Harms Employee Health and Company Performance—And What We Can Do About It*. New York: Harper-Collins, 2018.

Pfeffer, Jeffrey. *The Human Equation: Building Profits by Putting People First*. Boston: HBS, 1998.

Pink, Daniel H. *Drive: The Surprising Truth About What Motivates Us*. New York: Riverbed, 2009.

Sandberg, Sheryl and Adam Grant. *Option B: Facing Adversity, Building Resilience, and Finding Joy*. New York: Knopf, 2017.

Sinek, Simon. *Start with Why: How Great Leaders Inspire Everyone to Take Action*. New York: Penguin, 2009.

Sullivan, Gordon R. and Michael V. Harper. *Hope Is Not a Method: What Business Leaders Can Learn from America's Army*. New York: Crown, 1998.

Wheatley, Margaret J. *Turning to One Another: Simple Conversations to Restore Hope to the Future*. San Francisco: Barrett-Koehler, 2002.

Zimmerman, Brenda, Curt Lindberg, and Paul Plsek. *Edgeware: Lessons from Complexity Science for Health Care Leaders*. Irving: VHA, 1998.

ACKNOWLEDGMENTS

As I referenced in the section "Mentors Everywhere," the mindful, attentive leader is surrounded by individuals in their life from whom they can learn, grow, and experience support. I have had many mentors in my lifetime.

My first mentors were my family. I was blessed to have parents, John and Lois, who provided unconditional love and support and always emphasized the importance of family and education. My sisters, Marcia and Judy, showed unwavering patience and love in dealing with a challenging little brother. My son Ryan and grandson Taylor bring such joy and energy to my world, and I relish their love and watching them live their lives with substance and compassion. And finally, I include Father Ed Ostertag, who was like a surrogate uncle to me, a loyal and supportive friend and mentor for fifty years.

In school, my teachers made an impact, and I am grateful to many, including Richard Klinck, whose impact as a sixth-grade teacher was long enduring, and also my junior high school teacher and coach, Bob Linnenberger, and high school teacher, Helen Knudson.

During my university political science studies, I was exposed to Professors Cefkin and McConnell, who represented liberal and conservative belief and ideology with clarity and impact but also deeply respected each other's positions and right to support them. They emulated respect and open debate as the way to express differences.

The tone of my medical school experience was set by the Pediatrics Department led by Drs. Henry Kempe and Henry Silver. They taught the science well but modeled the role of healer and emphasized compassion and humanity.

During my surgery training, my professor of plastic surgery, Dr. Dave Dibbell was a hands-on, at-your-side teacher whose standards were high, while his ability to teach us how to think and problem solve was unique. Early in my practice, I was able to work with Dr. Chris Weatherly-White, who also had a very deep dedication to teaching and research.

Over the years, I had the good fortune to work with a

number of great surgeons, including Royal Gerow, Berry Morton, Bill Brown, David Charles, and Brad McDowell.

My nursing colleagues have also proven to be great mentors, and I have learned as much from my nursing partners as any group. Among the many partners and friends, I salute Ginnie McClain, Deb Zuege, Debbie Lantz, Lynn Bryant, Judy Morahan, Julie Mummaugh, Linda Fiske, Debbie Sacks, and Denise Black-Anderson.

I have also benefited from the lectures, writing, and conversations with business school professors such as Amy Edmondson, Jeffrey Pfeffer, Merwyn Hayes, and Jim Collins.

Many organizational leaders contributed to my learning, including, from Institute of Healthcare Improvement: Maureen Bisognano, Don Berwick, and Derek Feeley; from Alliance of Community Health Plans: Tricia Smith, Lynne Cuppernull, Ceci Connolly, and the board and medical directors; from American Medical Group Association: Don Fischer, Jerry Penso, Ryan O'Connor, and their strong board; and from National Quality Forum: Christine Cassell and Helen Darling.

I have a long and growing list of global leaders to acknowledge, including Lord Ara Darzi, Nicolaus Henke, Thomas O'Dowd, Ronan Fawsitt, Tim O'Connor,

Walter Kmet, Alison Verhoeven, Lord Victor Adebowale, Tim Fountaine, Charlie Taylor, Ellen Feehan, Brindan Surtesh, Egbert Schillings, Jochem Overbosch, Nav Chana, Charles Alessi, George O'Neil, Ben Richardson, David Colin-Thome, Chris Goodey, Chris Ham, and Emmet Kerin.

There are so many Kaiser Permanente leaders and physician leaders to acknowledge that any attempt at a list would undoubtedly and unintentionally omit too many, but please know that I am forever indebted to the contributions and friendships so many valued and respected colleagues have made to my professional career.

So while I will surely miss someone, I am grateful to Permanente Medical Directors: Rich Isaacs, Ed Ellison, Robbie Pearl, Jeff Weisz, Geoff Sewell, Bill Wright, Rob Schreiner, Andy Lum, Margaret Ferguson, Imelda Dacones, Mary White, Bernadette Loftus, Steve Tarnoff, Oliver Goldsmith, Michael Kanter, Paul Minardi, Scott Young, Bill Marsh, David Bell, Jeffrey Grice, and Amy Compton-Phillips.

In addition to strong Permanente physician leaders, I also benefited from strong executive support, including Ilene Moore, Chris Grant, Pauline Fox, Claire Tamo, Hal Wolf, Amy Lou, Nancy Taylor, Heather Hanson, Glen Hentges, and Jennifer Holguin.

In an organization like Kaiser Permanente, much of the success depends on a healthy partnership between the Permanente Medical Groups and the Kaiser Foundation Health Plan. Again, at the risk of missing wonderful colleagues, I acknowledge George Halvorson, Bernard Tyson, Kathy Lancaster, Artie Southam, Paul Swenson, Ron Copeland, Chuck Columbus, Greg Adams, Ben Chu, and Donna Lynne.

I have learned and gained support from many incredible physician leaders, and here is just a short list: Gary Kaplan, Rob Nessee, Denis Cortese, Bob Margolis, Don Berwick, Lord Ara Darzi, Glen Steele, Toby Cosgrove, Brent James, David Howes, Paul Grundy, Doug Eby, and many more dedicated leaders.

And finally, I would like to make three special acknowledgments. First, to Susan Paul, who has been the steady ears and eyes to help me go from ideas to substance on so many topics to make this book happen. Second, to Charlie Kenney, who patiently worked with me to coauthor our book, *The Doctor Crisis*, which taught me so much about writing. His patience with my shortcomings was invaluable, and during that experience, Charlie became a valued mentor and true friend.

And finally, to Heather Hanson, Ph.D., who provided me and the writing process with content, criticism, and direction at different times. I leaned on her important expertise and experience when the messages were not fully clear.

ABOUT THE
AUTHOR

DR. JOHN "JACK" COCHRAN, MD, FACS, served as Executive Director and CEO of the Permanente Federation, the national organization of Permanente Medical Groups, from 2007 to 2015, where he led innovations in care delivery and major improvements in clinical quality. He has also served as President, Executive Medical Director, and Chairman of the Board of Colorado Permanente Medical Group from 1999 to 2007 and established its Department of Plastic Surgery. *Modern Healthcare* named Dr. Cochran one of the Fifty Most Influential Physician Executives in Healthcare in 2009, 2010, and 2012.

Under Dr. Cochran's leadership, Kaiser Permanente implemented an electronic health record, the largest successful nongovernment clinical information systems deployment in the world. The organization was recognized as a national leader in clinical quality by multiple institutions, including the Medicare Star Programs and the National Committee for Quality Assurance (NCQA). When Cochran retired from his leadership at Kaiser Permanente, the organization had grown to ten million members and twenty thousand physicians.

Dr. Cochran leveraged his speaking and teaching skills regarding global health care transformation and physician leadership when he worked with Congress and the White House from 2008 to 2010 to draft health reform legislation. He addressed reform at the 2010 National Governors Association Annual Meeting; testified before the Congressional Committee on Health, Education, Labor, and Pensions in 2009; and presented at the Senate Finance Committee's 2008 Health Reform Summit.

Dr. Cochran earned his medical degree from the University of Colorado School of Medicine and served residencies at Stanford University Medical Center and the University of Wisconsin Hospital. He is board certified in otolaryngology (head and neck surgery) and in plastic and reconstructive surgery. He practiced plastic and reconstructive surgery at St. Joseph Hospital in

Denver from 1981 to 2007, where he also served as Chief of Surgery, President of the Medical Staff, and was a member of the Hospital Board of Directors for two terms.

While CEO of the Permanente Federation, Dr. Cochran served on the boards of the Alliance of Community Health Plans, the American Medical Group Association, and the National Quality Forum. He has written many articles and blogs, contributed chapters, and is the coauthor of *The Doctor Crisis: How Physicians Can, and Must, Lead the Way to Better Health Care*, with Charles C. Kenney.

Since 1981, Dr. Cochran has volunteered his reconstructive surgery and consulting services in Nicaragua, the Philippines, Ecuador, Tanzania, and Nepal. He also served as President of the Consortium for Community Centered Comprehensive Child Care (C6), whose focus was to assist the fundraising and construction of two hospitals in Tanzania.

He developed the Cochran Family Professorship in Science at Colorado State University, is a Presidential Scholarship supporter at the University of Colorado School of Medicine, and serves on the boards of directors of UC San Francisco Global Health Group, University of Colorado Foundation Board of Trustees, and Clarify Health Solutions.

Dr. Cochran lectures globally on transforming health care with a focus on physician leadership.